PETRARCH

Everywhere a Wanderer

CHRISTOPHER S. CELENZA

REAKTION BOOKS

For Karl Kirchwey

Published by Reaktion Books Ltd
Unit 32, Waterside
44–48 Wharf Road
London N1 7UX, UK
www.reaktionbooks.co.uk

First published 2017
Paperback edition first published 2022
Copyright © Christopher S. Celenza 2017

Printed and bound in India by Replika Press Pvt. Ltd

A catalogue record for this book is available from the British Library

ISBN 978 1 78914 673 8

COVER: Justus van Gent, *Petrarch*, 15th century, oil on panel.
Galleria Nazionale delle Marche, Urbino – photo Scala, Florence
(courtesy of the Ministero dei Beni e delle Attività Cultural)/
Art Resource, New York

'Complexities of interpretation are food and drink to Petrarchan scholars, and Christopher Celenza tucks into them with quiet determination in his short life-and-works overview . . . Celenza's book introduces us to the breadth of Petrarch's intellectual world.'
— CHARLES NICHOLL, *London Review of Books*

'Celenza's account, easily the best and most accessible life of Petrarch to appear in English in a century . . . ranges easily over the whole of the poet's life and times, following him in the "wanderings" Celenza describes as characterising Petrarch's somewhat peripatetic career in the service of the wealthy Visconti family and others . . . The book's most memorable Petrarch is also its best achievement: the man himself, querulous, self-doubting, eager for fame but distrustful of it. That Petrarch very much does speak to our own age, and in these pages by Celenza, he finally gets a life of his own.' — *The National*

'[Petrarch] himself turned again and again in his writings to the flaws of humanity. Celenza exposes the Italian writer's flaws throughout his book, while simultaneously eliciting pity and respect. If he's a "misunderstood" man, then this book makes us want to understand him, contradictions and all.' — *Times Higher Education*

'The entire book shines with Celenza's close attention to historical and philological detail, his superb textual and contextual analyses, and his deep understanding of how much Petrarch's legacy contributed to European cultural life . . . Though designed for and accessible to a wide readership, the book will delight Petrarchan specialists with up-to-date nuggets of scholarly information, smart insights into cultural contexts, and powerful reinterpretations of landmark texts.'
— *Renaissance and Reformation*

CONTENTS

PETRARCHAE

Preface

EW FIGURES ARE AS MISUNDERSTOOD as Petrarch, or Francesco Petrarca, in the original Italian. His life spanned much of the fourteenth century, an epoch of turmoil and crisis, and he himself – in his interests and passions – responded in ways that made him famous in his own time and a landmark figure even now. Over the centuries since his death in 1374, however, much has changed regarding his reputation and identity (illus. 1).

If he is known today, it is for his love poetry, written beautifully and evocatively in the vernacular. Indeed, Petrarch's Tuscan poetry served as one of the models for 'high' Italian when later thinkers in the sixteenth century were fashioning the canon and vocabulary of what became the Italian national language. And Laura, the subject of most of Petrarch's poems and the animating impulse behind all, became over the ages, like Dante's Beatrice, a model of the idealized woman: not woman as a person with an inner life but woman as symbol of male desires, aspirations and inner turmoil. It is this Petrarch – Petrarch the Tuscan poet – with whom later ages developed a fascination.

Yet during Petrarch's lifetime, he considered his work written in Latin more important. He wrote numerous Latin

1 Justus van Gent, *Petrarch*, 15th century, oil on panel.

letters, which he collected and quite deliberately curated, reflecting a wide network of friends. He made trips to obscure libraries, so that he could find and study Latin works little known to the Middle Ages. In his continued cultivation of Latin, Petrarch set the tone for the rest of the Italian Renaissance, whose leading lights after him continued the quest to rediscover the ancient Roman, and eventually Greek, worlds in all their fullness. If every major Western city is full today of classicizing architecture, this tendency is due in no small part to the passion for Graeco-Roman antiquity that Petrarch inaugurated. If classical authors like Virgil, Cicero, Livy and eventually a whole host of ancient Graeco-Roman writers emerged as the centre of school curricula for many centuries, this development, too, can be traced back to Petrarch. Though he was by no means the first thinker to develop a consuming passion for the ancient world, he was the first one to make it a cultural ideal that had staying power. And he did so in a way that can seem paradoxical at first glance: by adapting it to his age with his own, very specific Christian sensibility.

When all is said and done, there have been three different images of Petrarch, whose perceived importance has varied over time. First, there is Petrarch the Tuscan poet, whose fame has lasted and grown over the centuries. Then there is Petrarch the classicist who in looking backwards to antiquity pointed the way towards the Renaissance. Finally, there is Petrarch the Latin writer. This last identity, though so vital to him during his lifetime, was soon dissociated from his image as the classicizing 'father of the Renaissance'. New literary tastes, changing priorities among learned elites and blind spots among scholars all led to Petrarch's Latin writing sinking into relative oblivion. In life, however, Petrarch enfolded all three of those identities. To understand him in full, they all need to be brought to the fore.

Petrarch. A Tuscan who grew up in France. A devotee of the ancient pagan Roman world and a devout Christian. A lover of friendship and sociability, yet at times an intensely private and almost misanthropic man. A person who believed life on earth was little more than a transitory pilgrimage, yet one who nonetheless took himself as his most important subject-matter.

Who was this man?

ONE

Origins and Early Years

You will, perhaps, have heard something about me, although even this may be in doubt, since a small and obscure name will travel far in time and space only with difficulty. And it is likely that you will want to know what sort of man I was, or what was the fortune of my works, especially those whose reputation has reached you or of which you have at least heard the titles.[1]

ETRARCH WROTE this letter when he was in his sixties. In its vanity disguised as modesty, misanthropy masquerading as a love of the simple life, and willing revelation of what was clearly a complicated personality, his 'Letter to Posterity' is nothing less than a classic.

The letter is indeed addressed simply to 'posterity' – not to a specific person but to an unnamed and unquantified readership, who might, someday, take an interest in Petrarch. *If you have heard of me, you might like to know something about what I was like.* Here Petrarch (now a relatively old man, of course) reveals that his substantial fame will outlive him.

Petrarch was exceptional, in all the senses that word implies. One manifestation of this exceptional status is that, unlike many medieval thinkers, Petrarch took great care in shaping his own identity, often openly and unashamedly taking his own life as his subject-matter. He wrote a series of revealing letters in Latin, the most famous of which is the 'Letter to Posterity'. It uncovers much about Petrarch's personality and, to boot, offers an (admittedly short and sometimes attenuated) autobiography. For example, he tells of the circumstances in which he was born:

> My parents were honorable, Florentine in origin, and possessed of a middling wealth – or if I should speak truly – verging on poverty. They were expelled from our homeland, and so I was born, in exile, in Arezzo, in the year of this last age which began with Christ, 1304, at dawn on a Monday, the twentieth of July.[2]

Exile, here and elsewhere in Petrarch's work, is never far from the surface. Soon thereafter, in the course of the letter, Petrarch tells of the family's move to the city of Avignon. And it is here where we can, for now, take leave of the 'Letter to Posterity', so that we can look more closely at Petrarch's youth, and at the environment in which he grew up.

All indications show that he was a precocious boy, studying Latin with an elementary school teacher named Convenevole da Prato in Carpentras. Convenevole exposed Petrarch to Italian traditions of teaching and learning basic Latin grammar, rhetoric and logic. Thus, though in France, Petrarch had contact with certain Italian traditions. Carpentras, an otherwise unremarkable city, was noteworthy because it was near the French city of Avignon (illus. 2). Here then is another reason why Petrarch is exceptional, different: though known today as part of the Italian literary and intellectual tradition, he grew up in France. Understanding why this was the case offers us a window into the world into which Petrarch was born, a world of epochal, revolutionary change.

His family hailed from Tuscany and had roots in Florence, where his father, like his grandfather and great-grandfather, was a notary. Notaries represented something important in pre-modern Italy, and it is appropriate to pause briefly to focus on what that profession signified. Their various functions helped society run its everyday operations. If you needed a contract written, an important document drafted or an official record of a legal proceeding, you turned to a notary. Notaries received extensive education in basic Latin, were trained in certain formal aspects of rhetoric, and – importantly – were adept writers, in the literal sense: in the pre-modern world not all people who were literate were regular writers. Notaries could be entrusted with an official letter that needed to be written. They not only possessed the basic language skills to write but were well versed in the many formalities needed to make the actual physical document acceptable.

Notaries also embodied a long and distinctive tradition in north and central Italy, in the sense that they were laymen, meaning non-clerical and thus not tied formally to religious institutions. Deeply embedded in Italian traditions, in other words, there was a secular element, one with which many Italians had contact. In a world where few people could read and write, notaries held a special position, with a status that allowed them to have what was sometimes designated, in medieval Latin, as *publica fides* – 'the public trust'.

More than this, notaries possessed a skill, and they wrote with certain designated techniques, whereby corrections would be made in a characteristic fashion, the page would be blocked out in recognizable ways, and the formalities of writing possessed a kind of standardization. Scholars who have studied

2 Map of Petrarch's Vaucluse and surroundings, as imagined by Alessandro
Velutello in a 1547 edition of his commentary on Petrarch's Italian poems,
published by Gabriel Giolito in Venice.

Petrarch's own manuscripts – .works that he wrote by hand and that we are fortunate enough to possess – have noticed strong similarities to the notarial tradition.[3] Simply put, Petrarch's writing, which had to do with literature and scholarship, bore powerful traces of the formal procedures that notaries had developed. This deep family background, which he imbibed almost by osmosis, stayed with him his whole life. His early education, too, formed him in notable ways, taking place as it did in France.

Why was Petrarch in France, along with many other Italians? The basic reason was that his father, 'Ser Petracco', brought the family there to follow the papal court (illus. 3). 'Ser' was an honorific title, indicating a professional status of the sort that notaries possessed. And notaries were in demand at the

3 Wide panoramic view of the papal palace in Avignon, France, as it appears in modern times.

papal court, which was undergoing a series of changes at that moment. The most important of these was in its location. After a millennium of being located in Rome, the city where St Peter – the first bishop of Rome – had been martyred, the papacy's revolutionary relocation was nothing short of profound in its implications. The bishops of Rome had over time attained leading status in the early Christian Church, so much so that they had earned the title of 'Papa' – 'Pope'. Along with this title went prestige of place. Even before the rise of Christianity, Rome had acquired the nickname the 'Eternal City'.[4] As institutional Christianity set roots down there, one of the seemingly everlasting attributes added to the myth of Rome was the presence of the papacy, along with its official manifestation, the 'papal court'.

The *Curia Romana*, as the papal court was known in both Latin and Italian, developed and grew as the institution of the papacy flourished. By Petrarch's day the papacy had a twofold aspect: religious and political. Popes had gone from the representative of St Peter's authority to the living symbol of God on earth. Whereas in the early Middle Ages, popes took the title 'servant of the servant of God' (*servus servorum dei*), as Pope Gregory the Great (590–604) preferred to be known, by the twelfth century Popes instead were seen as the 'vicar of Christ' (*vicarius Christi*), the representative – in the sense of stand-in – of Christ on earth.[5] They were believed to possess a 'plenitude of power' (*plenitudo potestatis*) and saw themselves as political actors as well as religious figures. Moreover, the papal court developed alongside and grew together with the papacy in the Middle Ages, evolving along lines similar to those of other late medieval governments. By Petrarch's day the papal court consisted of a large staff of people, divided up into administrative, financial and judiciary branches. In this context, notaries like his father Ser Petracco were needed.

The move to Avignon occurred for a host of reasons, all of them related to the fact that the papacy was a player in European power politics. Ser Petracco's career and his move from Florence to France left a significant imprint on his son Petrarch, in two ways. The first, and more global, had to do with a cultural and political fact experienced by many: the move of the papacy to France. As a youth Petrarch experienced all of this at first hand, and like all children he internalized aspects of the larger sense of crisis that many European cultural elites experienced: a profound sense of instability, as the Holy Roman Church (*sacra romana ecclesia*, in Latin), the one stable, unifying factor in a time marked by religion, changed locations.

And there should be no mistake about it. On the one hand, in a time when there was neither mass transit nor mass circulation of written information, there were, surely, 'Christianities' at the local level, meaning that across the wide geographical area of Christendom, Christianity was practised and lived in different ways in different locations. The local Christianity of Alpine villages was different from that experienced in a metropolis like Paris, London or, indeed, Rome. On the other hand, the papacy and its centrality to organized, elite Christianity represented a rock on which people could rely, a long-lasting manifestation of the 'rock' on which Christ built his Church, St Peter, the quintessential Roman saint, martyr for the faith and the reason why the Church was located in Rome.[6] The life of a literate Christian was deeply entwined with a Christian identity, reliant on that identity's grounding in Rome and affected by the papacy's absence from the Eternal City. Petrarch, certainly one of these elites, experienced this dislocation as a youth, indeed grew up with it. His life experience encompassed this element, something that included, in a more personal and psychologically influential manner, the second way he was affected by his early time in France.

This second element, deeper, subtler and in some ways more powerful, had to do with a sense of exile that permeated Petrarch's psychology, inflected his writing and, in a larger respect, helped create a sense of 'Italian-ness' that had a long afterlife. Petrarch routinely signed himself and was addressed as 'from Florence'. For one example, we can highlight when he was offered a canonry – an ecclesiastical office that offered light duties and an income – in Gascony, a region in southwest France. In this case the letter of appointment was addressed to *Francisco Petracchi de Florentia*, or 'Francis, son of Petracco, of Florence'.[7] Since his father was a Florentine citizen, Petrarch too claimed this identity.

More than this, he also came to see 'Italy' as a potential unity (rather than the hodgepodge of independent city-states that it was in reality), one that could function as such if only it had the right leadership, leadership that needed perforce to be exercised from Rome. As we shall see, Petrarch saw himself as part of all of this, as a larger-than-life figure of historical importance and destined for great things. Part of this deeply felt identity included the strong sense that he was an 'exile', someone doomed to live far from his *patria* (his 'homeland', Florence), even as Italy as such loomed large, with its formidable ancient past and its period of empire behind it, but perhaps recoverable once more.

All of this – the way that exile permeated Petrarch's work, the alienated 'Italian-ness', the way that institutional Christianity formed part and parcel of Petrarch's identity – lay in the future. If we return to his youth and to the course of his life, we can see that Petrarch established a paradigm for a number of Italian intellectuals who came after him: he went to law school, only to drop out.[8] At his father's urging Petrarch attended the law school of Montpellier. Much later, in 1367, he looked back on the period with fondness, writing to a friend with whom he had attended Montpellier that the environment was ideal: 'what tranquility, what peacefulness, what wealth of merchants, what swarms of students, what an abundance of teachers!' The impression he received then, only a young teenager when he attended Montpellier, stayed with him, as did his impression of Bologna, his next major stop on the educational ladder. He recalled the 'great gathering of students, the order, the alertness, the majesty of the teachers'. And then, the highest compliment: 'you would have thought that the ancient jurists had come back to life.'[9]

In the interim between those two experiences, Petrarch's mother had died, and it is to this bitter experience that we owe his first preserved writing, a Latin poem in 38 hexameters, in which he declared, 'together you and I will live, together will we be remembered' and bemoaned the fact that he 'shed tears on her cold limbs'.[10] Her name in Italian was Eletta, and Petrarch used the Latin form of that name, *Electa*, in the poem, a word that means 'chosen', the 'elect' and so on. Did the early loss of his mother lead Petrarch to look for a woman to fill that place of longing?

His time in Bologna lived in his memory as a period of study, to be sure, but also as a moment of carefree youthfulness. It unfolded during the years 1320 to 1326 and included interruptions for trips back to Avignon. Petrarch was handsome and, during that period (he writes in a 1349 letter of reminiscence to his brother), vain and prone to love affairs. They both worried about their appearance, and Petrarch evinced a special fondness for well-made clothes.[11]

In his 1367 letter, Petrarch highlighted what his young life had been like, in the company of his friends. Though the letter is tinged with both nostalgia and a bit of crotchety 'back in my day' grumpiness, it is worth listening to what Petrarch says to his old friend about those long-ago student days: 'there lingers in my memory, and I believe in yours, a fixed, indelible imprint of that time when I lived there as one of the students; already a more passionate age had arrived as I entered adolescence and was more daring than I should have been and had been.'[12] We can pair this sentiment with what he says about the course of his life, in his roughly contemporary 'Letter to Posterity': *adolescentia me fefellit, iuventa corrupuit, senecta autem correxit* – 'youth deceived me, early adulthood seized me, but old age corrected me.'[13] 'Seized me': the Latin verb *corripuit* can mean many things, but for the most part it has to do with 'taking', 'plundering' or, as translated here, 'seizing'. Petrarch had a tendency later in life to look back on his younger years with a mixture of regret, longing and a tendency to compartmentalize, as if he were glad that all that youthful passion was behind him.

But it is also true to say that sex was never far from his mind. Petrarch, in fact, seems to have kept a sex diary, though diary may be too strong a word.[14] It is, instead, a list that indicates, without giving any detail, certain times when he may have engaged in sexual activity. Though he had two illegitimate children, he never named their mothers. And though he obviously engaged in sexual activity, he always saw it, as did his hero St Augustine, as a sign of weakness and disorder and as something to be shunned if one could. Those reflections, however, emerge later in his life. For now, we can return to his lengthy Bologna period. For during that time, in 1325 to be precise, Petrarch collaborated on a project with his father, Ser Petracco, to produce a manuscript that has become known as the 'Ambrosian Virgil'. Behind it there lay a series of stories and family dynamics that are worth bringing to the fore.

Petrarch's relationship with his father was complicated. Like other notaries of his time, Ser Petracco had literary interests that were consonant with the beginnings of the new Italian appreciation for antiquity. Petracco had a special interest in Cicero, for example, one that Petrarch inherited early on.[15] But like many parents, Petracco wanted to make sure his son had a viable career. He sent Petrarch off to Montpellier to study law when Petrarch was just a teenager, as we have seen. But Petrarch's own literary passions were never far from the surface. Very late in life, in another letter, Petrarch recalled that, as a young boy, he had jealously guarded all the books of Cicero, as well as of various poets, that he could gather, and that he had indeed been stimulated in these literary passions early on by his father. But then at a certain point – Petrarch does not specify precisely when – a signal event occurred:

Since all the books I had gathered of Cicero, as well as those of various poets, seemed obstacles to studies that would lead to a respectable income [he means the study of law] I saw all taken from the hiding places where I had stashed them and thrown into the fire, as if they were heretical books. Having seen this occur, I was tormented by it and groaned as if it were I who was burning. I remember that my father, seeing my sadness, snatched two volumes from the fire that were already somewhat burned. While I yet wept, he offered them to me, holding in one hand Virgil, in the other Cicero. Smiling at my sadness, he said: 'Here, take this one' – Virgil – 'as something to which you can occasionally turn to refresh your spirit, and take this other one' – Cicero – 'to help you in your study of law'.[16]

A number of factors stand out.

First, there is the fact that, though it was obviously his father who had thrown the books into the fire, in a passionate if perhaps extreme attempt to encourage his son to focus on his legal studies, Petrarch relates the episode in the passive voice: the books 'were taken' and 'were thrown'. It is as if Petrarch, even at that great distance, wants to protect his father, with whom (like a lot of young men) he disagreed but whom he loved dearly nonetheless. Second, it is clear that Petracco's was a literate household. Petracco spent quite a bit of time away from young Petrarch, since the papal court was in Avignon and Petrarch was raised in his early years in a nearby French town. But when they were together, Petracco's love of ancient literature left a strong imprint on the boy. Finally, the presence of Virgil and Cicero, the two great classics of ancient Latin poetry and prose, respectively, is meaningful if unsurprising. They left an imprint on everything Petrarch ever did, as he read and reread their works, imbibing them so thoroughly that passages drawn from them would pop up unbidden in his writing.

As to Petrarch's relationship with his father, they shared an interest in these authors and in Virgil especially, so much so that we can see that relationship manifested in a single book, one that Petrarch kept with him his whole life. This handwritten book now resides in the Ambrosian Library in Milan, having passed through many different hands in its storied history.[17] It contains texts by Virgil (the *Eclogues*, the *Georgics* and the *Aeneid*), the most famous ancient commentary on Virgil, by the late ancient commentator Servius, the *Achilleid* (story of Achilles) by the Silver Age author Statius, some poems by Horace, accompanied by commentaries, and a grammatical text by the ancient grammarian Donatus. It is, in its own way, a kind of mini-library. There has been debate over who compiled the manuscript, with some scholars suggesting that Petrarch, together with his father, was behind the collection, working on it when Petrarch was back in Avignon for a time on hiatus from Bologna and having hired an Italian, perhaps even a Florentine, scribe to copy the texts.[18] Others have proposed that Petrarch's father, when he was still in Florence and thus a contemporary of Dante, put the codex together.[19] Another scholar has suggested that it was copied in southern France, perhaps under Ser Petracco's direction.[20]

There is no doubt about one central fact: Petrarch added in his own hand roughly 2,500 marginal annotations to explain things in the texts. These annotations ran the gamut from brief lexical explanations in which this or that word was defined, to larger paragraphs linking the text under examination with other classics. Take, for example, his annotation to the *Aeneid*, Book One, line 36, a text that in Latin runs: *cum Iuno aeternum servans sub pectore vulnus* – 'then when Juno, nursing deep inside herself an undying wound . . .' (illus. 4). In the course of the *Aeneid*, here we are close to the beginning, after Virgil has invoked the muse and begun to unfold the tale of Aeneas. He is setting the scene for what is to come, and as he does so he introduces a major factor in the plot of the *Aeneid*: the goddess Juno, wife of Jove. Her hatred for the Trojans had emerged much earlier, when the Trojan prince Paris had picked Venus, over Minerva and Juno herself, in a beauty contest, and she had never let that 'undying wound' go. The epic hero Aeneas, of course, is himself Trojan, the son of a mortal, Anchises, and a goddess, Venus, who had bested Juno in the beauty contest. The narrative of the *Aeneid* sees Aeneas travel from the ruins of burning Troy, experience a number of adventures and, ultimately, arrive in Italy, where after a series of battles he succeeds in founding Rome.

Through it all Aeneas is observed and often hindered by the jealous goddess Juno, who wants to see him fail and who throws obstacles in his way whenever she can. This, then, is the context of that one little line, so seemingly innocuous when taken in isolation, so full of meaning however for Petrarch. In his comment on the line, Petrarch begins as follows: 'It is already from this point that the conflicts of the gods and their interventions in human affairs begin. Almost no part of this entire work, all the way up to the end, remains

4 Petrarch's annotation to Virgil's *Aeneid*, Book I, line 36, in his personal copy (sometimes known as the '*Ambrosian Virgil*'), *c.* 1340. See top left for the cited annotation.

untouched by them. In this respect Virgil followed Homer's lead most of all.'[21] Petrarch's commentary shows, first of all, that he has the whole arc of the *Aeneid* in mind and that he well knows that the *Aeneid* had, in its first half (books 1 to 6), Homer's *Odyssey* as background, and in the final six Homer's *Iliad*. Petrarch proceeds: 'Otherwise these discords that the gods invent, at least those which they are able – if there were a plurality of gods – point very strongly to one God, whom we too worship and whom the philosophers have been compelled to admit exists.'[22] Petrarch then alludes to passages in both Cicero and Aristotle that criticize the idea of a plurality of gods and that lean towards the notion of the existence of one supreme being. He ends by cross-referencing this note with two others throughout the manuscript.

So what do we learn? Most importantly, we learn that reading, for Petrarch, represented deep engagement. Even one line of a poem could lead down numerous pathways. Petrarch moves from the factual – this is the beginning of the gods' intervening in human affairs; Homer's epics served as 'deep background' for Virgil – to more subjective but nonetheless meaningful matters of interpretation. The big question (one that would loom ever larger after Petrarch) was: as a Christian how and to what extent could one engage with, learn from and incorporate into one's life pagan ancient texts? It is not that he is attempting to answer that question here. Rather, Petrarch's entire worldview is inflected by that question. In this instance, for example, we can detect, if not an anxiety about, at least a concern for the problem of polytheism. 'Gods' invent 'discords': this is the first problem. Gods are not truly divine, Petrarch is saying, if what they do mirrors human flaws and weaknesses. Instead, the very fact that these 'gods' are doing things unbefitting of divinity points, for Petrarch, towards the notion that there must, in the final analysis, be one God. And there are ancient precedents, even among pagan thinkers like Cicero and Aristotle, for thinking along these lines. Petrarch is alluding to a passage in Aristotle's *Metaphysics* where Aristotle suggests that there must be one first principle before all others.[23] And there are number of instances in Cicero where the idea of a plurality of gods comes under critical scrutiny.[24]

Remember, too: this was one note on one line. In this single handwritten book there are roughly 2,500 such notes, of various dimensions to be sure, but each one a precious piece of evidence concerning how Petrarch read. What we see is that this deep, repetitive style of reading was something Petrarch possessed from his youthful years onwards. It never left him. This book, the 'Ambrosian Virgil', served as a companion to Petrarch throughout his life. It must have been particularly painful when it was stolen, as it was in the late 1320s. And Petrarch was clearly delighted when he recovered the stolen work in 1338, so much so that he did something that has endeared him to lovers of Italian painting everywhere: he commissioned a frontispiece to the book from the brilliant Sienese painter Simone Martini (illus. 5).

Martini (1284–1344), along with Giotto, Duccio and Cimabue, represents one of the key protagonists of fourteenth-century Tuscan painting. Today, if you go the Uffizi, Florence's renowned art museum, as you pass into its second room you face a painting of the Annunciation – that crucial moment when the Archangel announces to a startled Virgin Mary that

5 Simone Martini's illuminated frontispiece from the 'Ambrosian Virgil',
c. 1340.

she will bear the Christ Child. Simone Martini (along with a contemporary painter, Lippo Memmi) was that painting's author (illus. 6). What one sees is manifold: first, a tremendous emotional energy, highlighting the momentousness of the event; a very intense angel and a Virgin Mary only beginning to realize with what sort of responsibility she has been entrusted. Next, there is the fact that the panel is clearly a deluxe work, adorned as it is with gold leaf (the angel's words proclaiming Mary to be blessed are highlighted in raised gold leaf). Finally, just peeking through here and there, there is an exquisite use of colour, delicate and clear all at once, as one sees most especially in the Virgin's shawl, draped behind her on the throne. This large painting (originally done in 1333 as an altarpiece for a chapel in the Cathedral of Siena) has earned its place among the masterpieces of Italian painting.

The elements that most distinguish that work (the formal beauty and coherence, the use of colour) are shared by the tiny frontispiece in Petrarch's Virgil manuscript. And like the Annunciation altarpiece in the Uffizi, the frontispiece tells a story, a small masterpiece in its own way of the power of text and image together (see illus. 3). We see the poet Virgil, first of all, reclining, with a pen in hand and a book on his lap. He is in a sylvan landscape, with what seem at first to be shepherds – they are dressed as such – around him. One is pulling back a veil-like tent behind which Virgil sits. Below there are inscribed two sets of Latin verses, authored by Petrarch, that run as follows:

Ytala praeclaros tellus alis alma poetas
Sed tibi graecorum dedit hic attingere metas

Servius altiloqui retegens archana Maronis
Ut pateant ducibus pastoribus atque colonis

Sweet Italy, you are a land that nourishes
    outstanding poets
But it is this man [Virgil] who allowed you to reach
    the goals of the Greeks.
Servius, who reveals the arcana of Virgil of the
    high-flown words
So that they may show the way to generals,
    shepherds, and farmers.

The text and image work together both to reveal what is happening in the scene and to point the way towards how Petrarch saw himself.

As to the scene, the shepherd who is pulling back the veil is none other than Servius, author of the most famous ancient commentary on Virgil's work (a text that is included in the 'Ambrosian Virgil'). This juxtaposition of poet and commentator reveals the way Petrarch saw the enterprise of reading: as a never-ending project that demanded close study of the original, Virgil (who lies recumbent in the illustration), but that also needed the guidance of a respected ancient interpreter, Servius (who pulls back the veil). Petrarch's thousands of annotations throughout the book manifest and extend that same project, whereby reading, writing and reflection all joined together in an everlasting feedback loop. Virgil's works emerge as self-evidently useful: for generals, there is the *Aeneid*. Its many battle scenes, descriptions of heroic military virtue and realistic depictions of what

we would today call the psychology of war all combine to make it a text that can be useful to military men – but only, Petrarch's verse suggests, if correctly interpreted. For shepherds and farmers, Virgil's *Eclogues* and *Georgics* can serve a similar professional purpose: to enrich their work and life if they can be made to understand the essential messages.

By the time Petrarch had reached his early twenties, his basic reading habits were formed. Later in life, he penned a remarkable letter to Giovanni Boccaccio, who became an admirer and friend. In this letter, Petrarch described the way he read and the effect that reading certain works had on him:

6 Simone Martini and Lippo Memmi, *Annunciation with SS Margaret and Ansanus*, 1333, tempera and gold on wood.

I have read Virgil, Horace, Boethius, and Cicero. I read them not once but a thousand times; I did not run by them but lay down beside them; I brooded over them with every effort of my intelligence. I ate in the morning what I would digest in the evening; I imbibed as a boy what I would ruminate on as an older man. I have ingested these things in such an intimate way that they have become fixed not only in my memory but in my marrow, having become as one with my own intellect. The result is that, even if I never read them again for the rest of my life, they would certainly stick, having taken deep root in the deepest part of my spirit.[25]

Petrarch goes on to say that he knows these works so well that there are times when he cannot distinguish passages in them from his own thoughts and even some times when he cannot remember that they are indeed by other authors.

This striking section tells us much. It is no accident that after the act of reading is introduced, the central metaphors are those of eating and of consumption: 'ate', 'digest', 'imbibed' and, most interestingly, 'ruminate'. That last word (the Latin form Petrarch uses is *ruminarem*) meant what we mean when we use the word 'ruminate' but it had a more basic meaning in Latin (one suggested by our own word 'ruminant'), referring as it did to animals eating. Virgil, for example, in a text Petrarch knew well, used the verb to describe a cow eating grass.[26] The point is that Petrarch sees his own enterprise of reading and writing as so natural that it is almost pre-reflective, as natural as an animal taking nourishment.

Books had already assumed a central place in Petrarch's character by the time of his law school years. Later, there will be more to say about his love for books, his personal library and, most importantly, the way his passion for books led to important discoveries and revolutionary scholarly work. For now, we should catch up with young Petrarch, in the early to middle 1320s. From 1320 until 1326, with an intermittent hiatus or two, he studied law in Bologna. Together with him was his younger brother, Gherardo. And Petrarch was joined in Bologna by two men who would become lifelong friends. First there was Guido Sette, whom Petrarch had known as a boy and the person to whom that descriptive letter of 1367 was addressed, a letter that, alas, Guido never read, dying in that very same year. Like Petrarch, Guido was an Italian taken as a boy to southern France. Guido's origins lay in the Lunigiana region of Italy, relatively close to Genoa. And Guido, unlike Petrarch, later in life took a more openly careerist direction, eventually rising to become archbishop of Genoa in 1358. Though their paths diverged, they remained in contact by letter.

More important for Petrarch's own fortunes and development, it was also in Bologna that he met Giacomo Colonna, a member of one of Rome's most prominent families and one that had very close ties to the papal court. It was through Giacomo that Petrarch had an entrée into the orbit of the Colonna family, something that proved important, not only for the sake of friendship but for sustenance. In 1325 Petrarch received some small funds from the Colonna family.[27] Giacomo's brother, Giovanni, was a cardinal, and in 1330 Petrarch joined the cardinal's household, becoming a chaplain for the family, receiving an income and remaining in their service until 1337.

That latter period, the early 1330s, represented a time of discovery and maturation for Petrarch, as we shall see. Before that, however, two momentous events occurred in Petrarch's life, each of which served as an important punctuation mark between one phase of life and another. The first was the death of his father in 1326. Petrarch was in Bologna when he heard of his father's demise, returning thereafter to Avignon, along with his brother Gherardo. Finally, Petrarch did what he always wanted to do but could not, given paternal pressure: leave behind the study of law. In his 'Letter to Posterity', he characterized what he thought about the law and about his studies of the law in Bologna:

> I was a young man destined for a career of great profit, had I only persevered in that enterprise. But I abandoned that study as soon as I was bereft of the care of my parents. It is not that I didn't like the law's authority, which without any doubt is great and full of Roman antiquity – something that delights me. Rather, what deterred me was the fact that the practice of law has been ruined by the perfidy of men. And so, I was unwilling to dive into serious study of a subject that I would not have wanted to practice in a dishonest fashion and that, in truth, I scarcely could have practiced honestly even had I wanted to do so. And besides, if I had practiced it honestly, my 'purity' would have been seen as incompetence.[28]

No law, then, or professional lawyering would be in Petrarch's future after his father died.

We learn more than that, of course, from the just-cited passage. First of all, there emerges something of which an attentive reader may already have got a glimpse: Petrarch had a strong sense of his own distinctiveness as a person and was willing to flout conventional expectations. In another letter from later in life, Petrarch describes himself, in Latin, as *peregrinus ubique* – 'everywhere a wanderer'.[29] The word translated as 'wanderer', or *peregrinus*, can also mean 'pilgrim'. If most people had a home, Petrarch early on conceived of himself as never fully at home anywhere. If most people who had begun a solid professional education, buttressed and encouraged by the expectations of their parents, simply persisted in that field of study, Petrarch instead was different. Though he would later in life work in loose diplomatic capacities for those who supported him financially, his mission from his early twenties onwards was singular: to focus on himself, his creative writing and his scholarly work. All else was secondary, and he took jobs and accepted this and that professional status in furtherance of those self-directed aims.

Two generations later, an astute intellectual named Leonardo Bruni (1370–1444) wrote a short 'Life' of Petrarch in Tuscan.[30] Bruni commented on the fact that Petrarch had taken minor orders during this early period of his life. In practice what this meant was that Petrarch was able to 'count' as a clergy member but would not advance to the full priesthood if he did not choose to do so. It also meant that he could receive certain financial benefits, called benefices, that were attached to various offices.

To give just one of a number of examples in Petrarch's life, in 1335 he was appointed 'canon' of a cathedral in Lombez, near Toulouse, though he never went there to live. It offered him a small income and the status of being a 'member' of the chapel. But it did not include what his contemporaries called the 'care of souls', or *cura animarum*. When Bruni commented on the fact that Petrarch had taken orders, he said that Petrarch had done so 'not so much by his own choice as constrained to it by necessity'.[31] Bruni was astute and, to an extent, he was right: Petrarch's inheritance from his father had been either mismanaged or embezzled or a bit of both, so that, as he said to his brother in a letter, 'from being rich we became poor.'[32] From the death of his father onwards in his life, Petrarch would seek emolument and support so that he could engage in one of his two great loves: the life of the mind, expressed in a classicizing and, as he aged, an increasingly Christian key. Though Bruni was right about the practical reasons behind Petrarch's taking of religious orders, Bruni's 'Life' missed almost entirely Petrarch's deeply interior Christian tendencies. By Bruni's day, Petrarch's Christian turn was all but forgotten by many leaders in the humanist movement that he did so much to animate. There will be more to say about Petrarch's religiosity later. For now, however, another event takes pride of place, one that led to Petrarch's second great, lifelong love.

His father gone, Petrarch returned to Avignon. Petrarch tells us what happened, and though the testimony is from later in his life, it is revealing for many reasons: 'Laura, celebrated for her virtue and long made famous in my poems, first appeared before my eyes in the early years of my young manhood, in the Year of Our Lord 1327, on the sixth day of

April, in the Church of Saint Claire in Avignon . . .' This notice about when and where he first saw 'Laura' occurs in the flyleaf of one of Petrarch's favourite books, the 'Ambrosian Virgil'. He wrote it after hearing of her death in 1348 from the bitter plague that passed through all of Italy, indeed all of Europe, from 1348–52. The note goes on to retell how he learned of Laura's death (in a letter from a friend) and, tellingly, why he wrote it down in this book:

> I decided to write down the harsh memory of this painful loss, and I did so, I suppose, with a certain bitter sweetness, in this very place that so often passes before my eyes, that it might remind me, owing to the frequent sight of these words and to meditation on the rapid passage of time, that there is nothing in this life in which I can any more find pleasure and that it is time, now that the strongest link to this place has been broken, to flee from Babylon . . .[33]

Petrarch wrote this little note most likely in 1351. In the 'Ambrosian Virgil' flyleaf, it forms part of a series of death notices in which Petrarch wrote down brief memorials when he heard of the deaths of friends and intimates. His memory of Laura, along with his other death notices, show his consciousness of the presence of death, even as they consequently evince his appreciation for life: how it is used, how one should conduct oneself in society and what place one's own interior life has in relation to one's identity.

Petrarch's notice of Laura's death also offers a sense of the impact she had on his life. Or rather, it reflects the way in

which, soon upon seeing a real, living, breathing woman with
an interior life, a place in the world and an intellect and emotions of her own (in short, a person), she became for Petrarch,
not Laura, but 'Laura' – his muse, someone who could do no
wrong, and someone who, of necessity, needed to be a perfect
representation of all the virtues traditionally attributed to
women (illus. 7). She was beautiful, she was chaste and she
was – most tellingly – silent. This latter quality is one that
Petrarch does not consciously evoke, and there are places in
his poetry where a fictive version of Laura is allowed a few
words. But throughout all his work, one has the sense that
Laura is an object rather than a person with subjective experiences of her own, someone who exists, in Petrarch's own
special conjuring, as something to look at and by which one
might be inspired.

It is also meaningful that Petrarch's sentiments regarding
Laura span his Latin and Italian works, even as they have different complexions in those two realms of writing. The note
in the 'Ambrosian Virgil' flyleaf is in Latin, the language
that, in some paradoxical respects, Petrarch considered most
natural when it came to matters of basic self-expression,
whether these emerged in letters, prose treatises or marginal
notes. Latin was so basic and important to him that there
were probably concepts and formulations that he could think
only in Latin.

Yet Laura – or, again, 'Laura' – is present so deeply in his
Italian poetry that she serves as a central point in his poet-
ics and thus also in the history of literature. There are, for
example, countless instances of her name serving as a building
block for his work. The word 'Laura' is related to the Italian

chogni uil cura mi leuar dintorno
et piu colei lochui bel uiso adorno
di ben far chosuoi exempli minnamora
Ma chi penso ueder mai tutti insème
per affalirmi or quindi or quinci
questi dolci nimici chio tanto amo
amor chon quanto sforzo oggi miuinci
et se non chal disio cresce laspeme
io cadrei morto oue piu uiuer bramo

O auro sempre in odio la fenestra
onde amor mauento gia mille strali
per che alquanti di lor non fur mortali
che bel morir mentre lauita è destra
mal forastar nella prigion terrestra
cagion mè lasso dinfiniti mali
et piu miduol che fien meco immortali
poi che lalma dalcor non si scapestra
Misera che dourebbe essere accorta
per lunga experienza omaicheltempo
non è chi indietro uolga ochi laffreni
piu uolte io chon tal parole scorta
uattene trista che non ua per tempo
chi dopo lascia esuoi di piu sereni

SI tosto come aduien che larco scocchi
buon sagittario di lontan discerne
qual colpo è da sprezare et qual dauerne
fede chil destinato segno tocchi
similemente elcolpo de uostri occhi

[marginal annotations, illegible cursive notes]

7 Illustration of Petrarch being pierced by an arrow emanating from
Laura's gaze, from a 1470 codex of Petrarch's *Canzoniere* and *Trionfi*,
published by Vindelino da Spira in Venice and illuminated by
Antonio Grifo (1430–1510).

word *lauro*, or 'laurel'. The image of the laurel tree served as a powerful presence throughout Petrarch's poetry. It was tied to the myth of Daphne and Apollo, told in inimitable fashion by Ovid (43 BCE–17 CE), whose *Metamorphoses* gathered together ancient myths in beautiful Latin verse and in an iconic fashion. It was a text that was well known in the Middle Ages and which was close to Petrarch's heart.

The myth of Daphne and Apollo occurs in Book I of the *Metamorphoses*, and it enfolded elements that became permanent parts of Petrarch's poetic vision: the helplessness of the lover, the rich interpenetration of nature and human life, and the distress that love can cause.[34] The myth runs as follows: Daphne is the daughter of a river god, unmarried and happy to remain so. Apollo, son of Jove and a god himself, speaks arrogantly to Cupid, god of love, who in revenge strikes Apollo with an arrow. This arrow, when it strikes someone, causes him or her to fall helplessly in love. And Apollo, when he sees Daphne, falls prey to precisely this sort of love – a madness, really, where all semblance of reason is lost. The love that Apollo feels for Daphne is, in Ovid's telling, like a fire that consumes hedges to which a passer-by's torch has been brought too close. The god finds her, and he tries to explain what and who he is: Jove is his father, he has the power to see the future, he is also the god of music, and so on. But to no avail: stubborn Daphne wants to preserve her virginity and remain single. She flees, and that flight impels him to chase after her. She runs through the woods: 'as the wind bared her limbs, as the breeze fluttered her garments, as a gentle gust of air set her soft hair streaming, she was all the more beautiful in her flight.'[35] But Apollo, young, strong god that he is, gives chase, and Daphne realizes that, with his divine speed and love-inflamed heart, he is bound to catch her.

Daphne's metamorphosis commences. Upon arriving at the river of her father, Daphne beseeches him to help her change form, to change 'that body which has given too much pleasure'.[36] She has barely finished her plea when her limbs begin to stiffen, her breasts are grown over with bark, her hair becomes leaves, her arms branches and her feet roots. In short, she becomes a tree. And not just any tree: a laurel tree. Apollo's love remains undiminished. He declares that this tree, the laurel tree, will become 'his' tree. Thereafter the laurel would be a symbol of music, of literature and of military triumph. Roman military generals who came back victorious in battle would wear a laurel wreath, as would distinguished literary figures, as would – as we shall see – Petrarch.

It is easy to observe, even from this one tale, why Ovid's *Metamorphoses* were beloved in the Middle Ages and why they held a special place in Petrarch's heart. Ovid's Latin is hypnotic, first of all, combining a stately hexameter with a talent for propulsive action. Along with Virgil and Horace, Ovid counts as one of the three most important poets of Rome's classical era. The *Metamorphoses* served also as a poetic compendium of Greek and Roman myths, many of which had at their centre transformations, explaining the origins of constellations, plants, trees, animals, rocks and so on. Whenever a plant was sacred to a god or had divine associations, this sacred character would be reflected in various ancient works. The handsome Adonis, for instance, with whom the goddess Aphrodite had fallen in love, was killed by a wild boar. So Aphrodite created a red flower, the anemone, from his blood.

Ancient literature is dotted with hundreds of these sorts of manifestations of the divine in the world. It was in the *Meta-morphoses* that one found explanations for these associations. Finally, the *Metamorphoses* summed up certain ancient attitudes about emotional matters, many of which remained similar in Petrarch's day, even though over 1,300 years had passed by then.

One such matter had to do with love. The tale of Daphne and Apollo in particular encompassed elements that, for Petrarch, permeated all of his poetry (illus. 8). When Apollo sees Daphne, he is so overcome that he loses his powers of reasoning, in effect. This belief about love entailed a number of assumptions: that love was a wild force, that it came from without, in a sense (symbolized in ancient myth by Cupid's arrow), and that it made the lover lose his or her rational faculties. As always, myths and beliefs help shed light on social practice. In this case these beliefs about love help explain why arranged marriages were the norm in both the ancient world and that of Petrarch (a practice that continued in the West until relatively recently and that is still practised in many parts of the world). Marriages existed to firm up ties between families, to solidify larger kin groups and to pass on property. The madness of love could not enter into that picture.

Petrarch was affected in many ways by this generally shared framework when it came to love. We can take, just as one example, his sonnet '*Voglia mi sprona*', or 'Desire Spurs Me On'. There will be more to say later about his poetry. For now, it is enough to know that in this poem Petrarch is trying to diagnose himself and to understand why he is so tormented by love. He writes that desire, love and pleasure drive him, even

: ſuol fare:iſcbuſilla i martiri
penſer cbe ſolo angoſcia dalle:
a dognaltro fa uoltar le ſpalle.
face obliar me ſteſſo a forza:
:n di me quel dentro & io la ſcorza.
cbe dal di cbel primo aſſalto.
iede amor moltanni eran paſſati:
:o cangiaua el giouinil aſpecto:
torno al mio cor penſier gelati
ʾauean quaſi adamantino ſmalto
entar non laſſaua el duro affecto.
ma ancor non mi bagnaua il pecto:
ʾmpea il ſonno:& quel cbe in me non era
areua un miracolo in altrui.
cbe ſon cbe fui.
a ʾl fin el di loda la ſera
:entendo il crudel di cbio ragiono
ɩ allor percoſſa di ſuo ſtrale
eſſer mi paſſato oltra la gonna:
: in ſua ſcorta una poſſente donna:

8 Illustration of Petrarch metamorphosing into a tree, from a 1470 codex of
Petrarch's *Canzoniere; Trionfi*, published by Vindelino da Spira in Venice and
illuminated by Antonio Grifo (1430–1510).

as his heart cannot recognize how an ever-present hope is a 'disloyal and blind guide'.[37] Then he writes: 'the senses rule, and reason is dead.'[38] Somehow he keeps hoping that there will be some sort of undefined consummation between him and his love object, a hope that one part of his soul recognizes as vain. And in case we are in any doubt about who this love object might be, we can turn to the poem's final tercet: 'One thousand three hundred twenty-seven, precisely / at the first hour of the sixth day of April / I entered into the labyrinth, and I see no way out.'[39]

The sixth of April 1327: the day he first saw Laura, as he memorialized in Latin in his prized Virgil manuscript, and as he makes clear here, in one of hundreds of lines of his poetry that reflect his anguished love and tormented personal identity. His sighting of Laura led to the discovery of love for Petrarch and to a new way of writing poetry, one that changed Western literature forever. But it is to another discovery that we now turn, a discovery that, in its own way, was equally momentous: the discovery of the ancient world.

TWO

The Discovery of the Ancient World

Y THE END OF THE 1320S, Petrarch was a vigorous, increasingly mature man. His parents were dead, he and his beloved brother Gherardo had run through the last of their inheritance, and Petrarch had to go about the business of finding financial support. He had taken minor orders and been employed by the Colonna family. It was in this time of his life, after the death of his father in 1327, that Petrarch's already existing passion for the ancient world changed into something more lasting and, in its own way, monumental.

It is a difficult thing for us to understand what the world of manuscripts – handwritten books – was like. If, today, we encounter a well-produced book, let's say a translation of the work of the ancient historian Livy, the format of the book itself tends to erase all that it took for it to exist in its current form. It will have a cover on which the author's name and the title of the work will be listed. It might also name the translator of the work and the editor, if those last two were different. But how did it get there? Perhaps the translator and editor will write notes about the text, commenting on things like what previous Latin edition it is based on, what previous translations have informed the current work, and what were the principles behind the translation. They will list, likely, a bit of bibliography so that curious readers and scholars might follow up and read more specialized studies about the work in question. Overall, however, it will be a relatively 'clean' text, one that is based on centuries of erudite work: scholars will have come to certain conclusions about the Latin text, and the current translator will build on the work of his or her predecessors.

Now imagine, instead, that there was no translated version of the text and, more importantly, that there was no single standard edition of the Latin text. Instead there were only handwritten copies. Not only that: those copies of the Latin text that did exist and to which you had access were incomplete. And even when you had before you two copies of what was, arguably, the 'same' text, the copies diverged in certain respects. You might encounter certain passages that showed different word ordering, that manifested variant spellings and that were written in markedly different handwriting. That was the situation in which Petrarch found himself when he approached the text of Livy, the great ancient Roman historian active in the time of Augustus, who wrote the history of ancient Rome from its semi-mythical founding to his own era. The issue of translation would not have mattered to Petrarch, since Latin, as we have seen, was a language with which he had an intimate familiarity.

Still, the difficulties that he did face included the disordered and incomplete state of the texts, the existence of separate editions with variant readings of the 'same' source, and the widely different styles of handwriting. All of this would have been familiar to Petrarch as he worked on Livy, who was quite important to Petrarch and his vision of the world. Petrarch saw Livy as a kind of key that could, he hoped, unlock the door to ancient Roman culture and thus also serve as a gateway to the betterment of his own culture, which he often saw as fallen. Only remote antiquity could help modernity, in other words.

Petrarch developed a habit, as his life went on, of writing letters to long-dead ancient figures as a way of communing with their long-lost spirits. He wrote one such letter to Livy, late in life, but it expresses sentiments that from his early adulthood were consistent: 'I wish either that I had been born in your age or you in mine, had it only been permitted by the heavens.'[1] The reason? Petrarch is disappointed in his own era, in its neglect of the past and its failure to preserve worthy remnants of cultures gone by: 'We know that you wrote 142 books on Roman matters. You must have worked with such energy and such unremitting zeal. Now, of that entire number barely thirty exist.'[2] Petrarch goes on to bewail the morals of his own day, when people value only money and sensual pleasure. That latter, peevish sentiment was a tic that became ever more pronounced as he aged. But his knowledge of the text of Livy and of how much, in fact, had been lost is meaningful. Livy had indeed written his history, called *Ab urbe condita* – 'From the Founding of the City' – in 142 'books', which are more or less the size of novellas, about seventy to eighty pages each in a normal modern edition. They were circulated in sets of ten (called 'decades') or sometimes five ('pentads'), and by Petrarch's day most had been lost, just as he noted.

Today, we possess 35 books with a fragment of a 36th, and the fact that we do is owed in no small part to Petrarch, who brought together the thirty he was able to locate in a way that bespoke energy and commitment (the final five books and fragment of the sixth were discovered later).[3] Keep in mind that there was no standard edition and no repository for Livy's texts and that there was no appreciable medieval tradition of gathering Livy's decades together. They were circulated separately and were, in effect, separate volumes with separate textual histories.

So Petrarch managed to locate copies of the three surviving decades in his own day: the first (Books 1–10), which told of the semi-mythical origins of Rome and its early rise to regional power; the third (Books 21–30), which culminate in Rome winning the final Punic war against the North African general Hannibal; and the fourth (Books 31–40), which tell tales of further conquest and consolidation carried out by Rome, as its growing dominion expanded eastwards. Working in 1328–9, Petrarch himself intervened. He had a manuscript copied of the first decade and did a substantial part of the copying himself (roughly the final fifty pages are in his hand). The text of the third decade that he had found was from around a century earlier but was missing much of its final section. Petrarch again got to work, copying into the text as much of the missing section that he could find. And he found a relatively complete version of the fourth decade, all of which he paid a copyist to transcribe. All of these parts Petrarch then bound together into one manuscript, which still exists today and which, after passing through different hands over time, now resides in the British Library in London, with the shelfmark Harley 2493.

In its own humble way this manuscript is a thing of beauty, less because of any high-level artistic accomplishments embedded within it and more because of what it tells us about how Petrarch worked. To have a better sense of Petrarch's method, we can take a look at one example, typical in its dimensions and revelatory precisely because of how average it is (illus. 9). The case in point comes early in Petrarch's manuscript, on the second full page of what we now possess. In Livy's *History*, however, we are already in Book 3. The reason? In the time that intervened between Petrarch's work on this codex in 1328–9 and its entry into the British Library the first 'quire' (and the last, for that matter) went missing.

Even this fact – that books were composed of quires – can give a modern reader pause. Quires are collections of leaves of paper or parchment (treated animal skins) that are folded, bound together and then sewn together into the format of a book. If you look closely at the binding of this book (unless you are reading it in a digital format), you should be able to distinguish the quires. Today they are more often pasted directly onto a binding, rather than being sewn together and then attached to a binding, as they were in Petrarch's day. And we don't use parchment at all anymore, needless to say, with paper being the norm. Paper (made of macerated rags) existed in Petrarch's day and cost about one-sixth the price of parchment. But Petrarch's Livy is a parchment book and, though bound together into one volume, a kind of composite book, one that reflects the taste and priorities of the person who had it bound (in this case Petrarch) as much as it does the vision of the original author. The fact that the book as we have it now is missing two quires also teaches us a lesson in the relative precariousness of early books: we are lucky, in other words to have what we do have, even as we lament what we have lost, much as had Petrarch himself.

If his work involved practical tasks like supervising how the quires of a manuscript should be selected and bound, it also – to return to our example – involved close reading and comparison. The case in question comes up in Livy's Book 3 (3.60.2). Rome has been founded, the period of the early

9 Annotated page from MS London, British Library, Harley 2493, f.2r. Petrarch's personal copy of Titus Livius, *Ab urbe condita*, c. 1329.

kingships is over and now the very young republic is trying both to figure out its political arrangements at home and to continue waging war and expanding its reach and power outside of the city. By this point Rome had established some of the policies that buttressed the young republic, the most important of which was the election every year of two consuls, militarily prominent men and co-leaders who would be responsible for the city's governance. But there had been a period when it seemed best to choose ten men to rule temporarily, in order to codify Rome's laws. They were called the *decemviri* ('the ten men'), and they took office in 451 BCE, by our current reckoning. As a group, they drafted a set of laws as they had been mandated to do, but they then overstepped their power. Finally, they were removed. Though a sense of political normalcy had been restored, they had done damage to the morale of the Roman military class and their troops. It is at this point in Livy's narrative that the example in question occurs.

Though this example is a simple matter, it shows with clarity both how Petrarch worked and what the stakes were in his textual labours. The immediate context is as follows: the two consuls then in power felt confident enough in how governance had been restored in Rome that they were ready, generals that they were, to take their troops back into battle, outside the city of Rome. One of them, named Valerius, faced the armies of two groups of people, known as the Aequi and the Volsci, who had joined together in in their enmity towards Rome. Valerius decided not to engage them immediately in battle. Livy judges this to have been a wise tactic, since, had Valerius engaged them, '*I do not know whether, given that the spirits* of the Romans compared to those of the enemy were so different owing to the ill-starred dealings of the decemvirs, there might have been a significant defeat.' The key part of the sentence, in italics (and here translated literally and in roughly the word order of the Latin in order to bring the following point into relief), runs in Latin as follows: *haud scio an, qui tum animi*. In the copy of this text that Petrarch had and of which he needed to make sense, the Latin ran *aut socio antiquum animalibus*, something like 'either the ally's ancient with the animals'. The reading in Petrarch's copy, in short, makes nonsense out of Livy's subtle point, to wit: Roman military morale was so low, owing to the unfortunate two-year rule of the *decemviri*, that the soldiers were not ready to face a foe.

This point is only one instance in Livy's large, sprawling history, and a relatively small one at that. Looking only at the faulty manuscript before Petrarch's intervention, a reader would have gleaned, of course, that Valerius did not then and there engage the Aequi and the Volsci in battle; and that very same reader would thus have had the basic events and chronology of the narrative. Missing, however, would have been that little bit of psychological artistry that Livy had injected with only a word or two: the morale of a military force is important when decisions are taken regarding when and where to go into battle. Again, only one point.

But imagine hundreds of such points, and hundreds of such corrections that Petrarch carried out – which he did – by comparing this one manuscript of Livy with others that he was able to find, thinking through the problem and the passage at hand, and then, finally, correcting the text itself (illus. 10). The marks you see in the illustration's third line are quite typical: dots are placed under the faulty words, alerting a reader that these are words in need of correction. Looking at the manuscript also helps us see precisely how errors in copies were transmitted. Recall that the phrase in question ran: *haud scio an, qui tum animi*. Note in the illustration that, in the original, instead of *haud* ('not'), the manuscript read *aut* ('either'). Petrarch simply squeezes in the initial 'h' and subtly changes the final 't' into a 'd'. Note too that he changes the word *socio* ('ally') to *scio* ('know' as part of the phrase 'I do not know') simply by putting a dot under the first 'o'. And one can see how small was the difference between the words *animalibus* ('with the animals', the incorrect reading of the manuscript) and *animi* ('spirits', the correct reading to which Petrarch restores the text). A sleepy scribe, a few letters here and there, and there you have it: a small incorrect reading is inscribed, to be copied again, and again, and again . . .

Petrarch was neither the first, nor would he be the last, to realize that there were better and worse readings in the world of handwritten texts and that to improve poor readings you needed to compare other texts, use your own common sense and try to piece together the best readings possible. Under the rule of the emperor Charlemagne (*r.* 800–814 CE), a

10 A closer look at an annotated page from Petrarch's personal copy of Titus Livius, *Ab urbe condita* (Btitish Library, Harley 2493), *c.* 1329, Parchment codex.

movement flourished to improve biblical and other sacred texts. And in the twelfth century a new appreciation for the classical world led to some similar textual scholarship. Petrarch's distinction, however, came in the way he unified a series of discrete ideas and predilections into one vision in what can only be described as an obsessive way. Love for the classical world, close attention to texts and a fine literary critic's eye for nuance all combined with his growing sense that his own soci-ety – in its values and in its basic language – did not 'match' that of the ancient Romans. His discoveries and his historical and scholarly work, in other words, fuelled each other.

To see how this reciprocal process worked, we can take a look at another of his 'discoveries', that of Cicero's oration *Pro Archia*, in the Belgian city of Liège in 1333. By this time, Petrarch was in the employ of the Colonna family and found himself travelling with them as they fulfilled their various obli-gations. But he was always on the lookout for books. Describing this period of his life in a later letter, Petrarch wrote that when friends, setting out to travel, would ask him what they could provide for him from their home countries, he had only one thing to say: 'nothing else but books, and especially those of Cicero.'[4] In that same letter (written when he was an old man) he tells of stopping in Liège, though he was on a journey with friends: 'I stopped there and I kept my friends waiting until I could have one of Cicero's orations copied by the hand of a friend and another by my own. Afterwards I circulated it throughout Italy.' One of these was Cicero's *Pro Archia*. As Petrarch explained, even copying the texts was not as easy as it would have been elsewhere: 'This will make you laugh. In that good but uncivilized city, it took quite a bit of work to find ink, and the ink I did find was practically the color of saffron!'[5] But find ink Petrarch did, and through his efforts Cicero's *Pro Archia* made its way into a wider circulation than it had previously enjoyed. Think about this fact: only two manuscripts of Cicero's *Pro Archia* survive from before Petrarch's time. There are over two hundred manuscript copies today, almost all of which 'descend' from Petrarch's copy (meaning that they were copies or copies of copies thereof).

Petrarch's discovery of Cicero's *Pro Archia* was important for a number of reasons. First, it showed Cicero in action, speaking in defence of a poet named Archias who had been accused of not being a citizen of Rome (seemingly a trumped-up charge made for political reasons). Petrarch and his emerging cohort of humanists admired Cicero greatly as a model of how to write Latin well. In this oration one sees Cicero summoning all of his vaunted eloquence and doing so in defence of a poet, no less. Even more important was what Cicero said and how he marshalled arguments. In explaining that he was arguing for Archias, the poet, Cicero said that, though Archias did not possess the kind of rhetorical eloquence that an orator and advocate employed, his own art, poetry, 'counted', as it were, since 'in truth, all the arts which have to do with humanity possess a certain common link, and it is as if they are bound together, one with the other.'[6] After this short but potent defence of poetry, in which the Latin word *humanitas*, translated here as humanity, appears prominently, Cicero goes on later in the oration to suggest to his audience that he will be speaking in a slightly different way than is normal in a court of law, and he asks leave of his listeners to allow him 'to speak a bit more freely concerning the study of the humanities'.[7] The expression used here and translated as 'concerning the study of the humanities' runs in Latin as follows: *de studiis humanitatis ac litterarum*, literally, 'concerning the studies of humanity and of letters'.

In both quotations we can see the Latin word *humanitas* used in a way that is somewhat particular and that does not map completely onto our word 'humanity'. Two points come into relief if we want to understand Petrarch and how this word would have resonated with him. First, Aulus Gellius (active in the second century CE) explained what this Latin word meant. He suggested that *humanitas* went beyond a concept that distinguished human beings from animals and even superseded the idea of 'love for all human beings'. Instead, Gellius wrote, *humanitas* is 'what the Greeks call *paideia* and what we mean when we say "education" and "instruction" in the good arts'.[8] This is what Cicero meant, too, in the *Pro Archia*, when he used the word 'humanity' and, indeed, when he paired it with the word 'studies'.

Second, the expression translated above as 'studies of humanity' in Latin, in its most basic form, is *studia humanitatis*. This expression came to denote a set of five verbal disciplines: grammar, rhetoric, poetry, history and moral philosophy.[9] These disciplines were what humanists like Petrarch and those who followed in his wake employed to rethink their world. Petrarch and others did not always name them all in one place. In addition, Petrarch and most humanists who followed him deliberately took the posture of anti-institutional outsiders. Accordingly, they rarely tried to have these disciplines officially represented in universities in the way they came to study and to practise these predominantly verbal fields of endeavour.

But this set of fields was real and important, and it represented a shift towards matters that, Petrarch and others like him hoped, would have relevance in the world, rather than being dry academic subjects that were taught and learned simply because they were on a curriculum. It carried great weight that Petrarch found this stirring defence of disciplines towards which he was naturally inclined in Cicero, his favourite prose Latin writer. It was a moment that fused together discovery, the hands-on work of copying a text and the excitement of travel. There were many such moments in Petrarch's life, all of which reinforced his instinctive and ever-growing notion that there was something missing from his own society that Roman antiquity, if considered rightly, could supply.

Yet when Petrarch discovered Cicero's *Pro Archia* in 1333, one thing was still missing from his life experience: Rome itself.

> It is sad to say it, but the truth is that Rome is nowhere less known than in Rome itself. I deplore not only the ignorance (though there is nothing worse than ignorance) but also the way in which many virtues have disappeared and gone into exile, as it were. Who can doubt that, were Rome to know itself once more, it would rise again?[10]

Petrarch evinced this sentiment in a letter, later in life, to Giovanni Colonna (not his friend and patron of the same name, but a relative). What he meant was that there were signs everywhere of Rome's former greatness: its ruined monuments, its ancient history as preserved by Livy and others, its long-ago empire. But the city itself and the place it held in the world lagged sadly behind that ancient legacy. Understanding why and how Rome, as Petrarch saw it, fell so far behind entails looking at both the reality and the constructs Petrarch created.

First, as to the constructs, we can highlight a trip of the mind with only a glance towards Rome and an idealized Italy, a trip that hints at the passion to follow and to Petrarch's dual identity, exterior and interior, where outward stimuli often led him to psychological introspection. The year was 1336. Petrarch had been cultivating the Colonna family and beginning his career as a literary figure, courtier and part-time diplomat in the employ of his patrons. His brother, Gherardo, took another path when the family money ran out, eventually becoming a Carthusian monk. Petrarch admired his brother's Christian devotion, even as Petrarch was self-aware enough to realize that he could never embrace that austere style of life, appealing though it often was.

These tendencies, and a glimpse towards Italy, emerge in one of Petrarch's most renowned letters, often referred to as the 'Ascent of Mont Ventoux' or the 'Ascent of the Windy Mountain'.[11] The mountain in question is in Provence, in southern France, and Petrarch and his brother climbed it for that most common of reasons: because it was there (illus. 11). In the 'Ascent', lengthy enough to be a treatise on its own, Petrarch described this voyage and in so doing left another in a series of glimpses into his soul that still evoke an emotional response today.

Petrarch addressed the letter to one of his best friends, Dionigi da Borgo San Sepolcro, a priest who also served as

Petrarch's confessor. Petrarch explains that he had hoped to engage on this climb for years, since he had lived in the region since he was a small child, 'cast here by fate'.[12] The letter is a model of self-examination, setting a tone that would weave its way in and out of the work of various thinkers over the succeeding centuries and culminate in the disarming *Essays* of Michel de Montaigne in the later sixteenth century, with their relentless autobiographical focus. But that moment was still far off when Petrarch wrote his letter and decided, simply, to tell his correspondent about himself and about his own inner emotional states.

11 The landscape of Mont Ventoux (in background).

He noticed the fact that his brother Gherardo took a straighter, but physically harder, route to the top: 'I had been attempting to avoid the annoyance of the ascent, but the nature of things does not depend on human inclinations, nor is it possible for any physical thing to go higher by descending.'[13] After some chuckling by his brother, Petrarch eventually reached the summit: 'From there I directed my gaze towards Italian realms, where my spirit most inclines.'[14] It is as if Petrarch is preparing himself mentally for Italy, for the real physical Italy he will visit in years to come.

Some introspection followed, Petrarch tells his confessor, and still, he regretted his continuing carnality, the fact that he could never free himself from physical weakness – from his love for Laura and his sins of the flesh, from his giving in to desires he would like to conquer but cannot: 'I shall hate if I can; if not, I will love unwillingly.'[15] Finally Petrarch looked outwards, seeing as far as the bay of Marseilles and looking down at the Rhone river.

Then, however, he took a look at a gift that his confessor had given him, a small copy of the *Confessions* of St Augustine, the book that had set the model, in the early fifth century, for an introspective autobiography, a Christian Latin classic from which Petrarch like many others drew spiritual sustenance: 'God – for he was present – is the witness that, where I first directed my gaze this was written.'[16] And here is the passage from St Augustine on which Petrarch alighted, by chance, he says: 'And men go to wonder at the mountain heights and the great waves of the sea, and the rivers' widest courses, and the ocean's circuits, and the way the stars revolve. But they do not consider themselves.'[17] Happening upon this passage, Petrarch writes, induced him to feel angry with himself ('I confess: I was stunned') for admiring earthly things when he should have been attending to the state of his soul: 'I turned my inner eyes upon myself, and from that moment there was no one who would have heard me say a word until we made it back to the bottom of the mountain.'[18] Preoccupied with himself and his own reactions, as ever, Petrarch then relates what he did, after he and his brother returned, with only the moon lighting their way, to the small inn from which they would depart the following morning:

> As the servants have been preparing dinner for us, I have gone, alone, into a hidden part of the house to write all of this for you, in haste and off the top of my head, so that my intention to write would not cool, as it might have done once I should depart.[19]

We observe signals both implicit and explicit in this letter, signals Petrarch intended for the readers who received it.

Who were these readers? There is the addressee, of course, Dionigi da Borgo di San Sepolcro, his friend and confessor. So in some ways Petrarch's self-scrutiny was entirely appropriate. But Petrarch was writing for other readers as well. He carefully collected his letters, preserving the things he wanted to preserve, so that he could leave behind an image of himself that he desired to foster. In this letter, what impressions would a reader receive? First, we see a Petrarch intensely concerned about the state of his own conscience and behaviour, scrutinizing himself for lapses and shortfalls, and exhorting himself to improve. One observes also a Petrarch committed to the idea of Italy, if not the reality, as he sighed for the 'skies of Italy', which he beheld with his 'mind, rather than with his eyes'. Finally, perhaps most importantly, there is Petrarch the writer, as he makes a point of telling Dionigi – and us – how and where he decided to write down his experiences. We see that writing served as an integral, almost therapeutic, part of his identity.

Petrarch made his most momentous trip, to Rome, in 1337 while still in the retinue of Cardinal Colonna. This was the great city of his imagination, where Cicero had lived and worked, the geographic basis from which, importantly, Rome had expanded and become the known world's greatest power in antiquity. Petrarch had been on a mission of discovery in books and, as in the 'Ascent of Mont Ventoux', in his mind. Now, it was time to turn to the physical reality. In his 'Letter to Posterity' he said that from his childhood he had 'always burned with a great desire to visit the city'.[20] In the same letter, Petrarch wrote that he had the chance on this visit to get to know Stefano Colonna, the patriarch of the Colonna family with which he was already so entwined, and a man 'who was worthy of being considered on par with the great men of antiquity'.[21]

The visit would leave him astounded. But the way he got there, and what he experienced along the way, are just as worthy of comment. The conditions can be summed up with a quotation from a letter Petrarch sent during his visit: 'In the final analysis, nothing is done here without arms.'[22] He sent that letter from Capranica, a town about 65 kilometres north of Rome, after he had settled in with Colonna relatives who lived there.

Having departed from the southern French city of Marseilles, Petrarch arrived by boat in the Italian city of Civitavecchia, a port city 67 kilometres northwest of Rome. The voyage was dangerous and stormy, and though he found a safe place to stay in Capranica, inland from the port, the conditions were unsafe outside the Colonna family compound. Petrarch remarked in that same letter that everyone seemed armed, and that he was continually warned not to venture out alone. Clearly awed by the natural beauty, he first described the hills, groves and springs with which he was surrounded. And yet:

> Peace alone has been sent into exile, and I know not what crime of the people, what laws of heaven, what fate or indeed what power of the stars makes this so. And what do you know? An armed shepherd watches over the woods, fearing not so much wolves but robbers . . . In the final analysis, nothing is done here without arms.[23]

What should have been a sylvan environment of peace and tranquillity, working in harmony with nature, emerges instead as a place of danger. He ventures out alone: 'Everyone looks at me with wonder, as I am calm, fearless and unarmed. By contrast I look at everyone with wonder, as they are fearful, agitated and armed.'[24] Petrarch concludes the letter by telling the addressee, Cardinal Giovanni Colonna, how he is looking forward to departing for Rome.

Yet it was still too dangerous, he related in an immediately succeeding letter, again to Cardinal Colonna. Petrarch reports that he had written to Giacomo Colonna, Bishop of Lombez and Giovanni's brother, for advice, given the danger. Giacomo, Petrarch states, wrote back enjoining him to wait there until Giacomo himself could come in person, which he did, arriving a few days later with his brother Stefano. 'They were attended by no more than one hundred horsemen each. The horror of the spectators was apparent, since they understood that there were five hundred or more soldiers under the flag of the enemy.'[25] But the two had reputations as good military leaders, and so, finally, Petrarch departed with them, despite the dangers.

His next and last letter in the sequence to Cardinal Colonna is indeed written from Rome. It is short: Petrarch says he is so overwhelmed that he cannot write more. He had feared that the Eternal City might not live up to the image he had built up in his mind, after so many years of dreaming of visiting the site of his greatest passion. However, he was not disappointed: 'Rome was, in truth, even greater than I had thought, and the ruins even greater still. I wonder no longer why the world was dominated by this city, but rather why I was dominated by it so late.'[26]

It is worth reflecting on Petrarch's first trip to Rome, as he recounts it. Much of his account in these three letters, written to the most prominent member of the family who were his greatest patrons, the Colonna, is unsurprising. His use of descriptive Latin language, classicizing and ornate, to relate his journey, combines with his palpable sense of anticipation at finally making his way towards Rome. Yet the conditions he describes might take a modern reader aback. Who were the 'enemies' of the Colonna whom the local inhabitants feared and who are depicted as blocking the way towards Rome? Why was this beautiful rustic area seemingly so dangerous?

The simple answer is that the enemies in question were members of the Orsini family, long-time rivals who would take any opportunity to harass the Colonna. The more complicated answer takes us perforce into the thorny world of pre-modern Europe and, at the same time, into Petrarch's political reality. If there is one characteristic that distinguishes this world from our own, at least in the relatively peaceful West, it is the presence of force and public violence. Petrarch's letters tell us that violence was not unexpected and that, to travel safely, an armed escort seemed a necessity. All of his work took place against this sort of background, and it led him, as it did many others, into a kind of dream state when it came to politics. Petrarch imagined an Italy that might once again be unified, as it had been in antiquity, and he became all too easily enamoured of dictatorial figures.

Writing about a year and a half after this trip, Petrarch's thoughts come through with great passion in his poem 'Spirto gentil', or 'Noble Spirit', which he wrote to an unnamed senator from Rome.[27] The poem alternates between recalling Rome's great ancient heritage of power – a point of pride – and focusing on its terrible current conditions – a point of shame. Petrarch addresses the unnamed senator as a 'lord strong, shrewd, and wise' who has now acquired the power to 'correct' Rome. He goes on:

I am speaking to you since nowhere else do I see a ray of virtue, which has been extinguished in the world. And I find no one who is ashamed of doing evil.

What it is that Italy waits or yearns for I do not know,
unknowing as it is of its own woes, old, idle and slow.
Will she sleep forever? And will no one ever awaken
her? Might I have my hand clutched in her hair![28]

Rome here is seen as feminine, and the unnamed figure is
seen as a potentially stern corrector of a sleeping, wayward
woman who needs to be awakened: 'put your hands into those
venerable locks confidently and into those unkempt tresses
...'[29] The woman is asleep, and the salvific figure needs first to
wake her up. Then: 'I, who bewail her torment day and night,
place the greater part of my hopes in you: for if the people of
Mars are ever to lift up their eyes to their own honor, it seems
to me that the grace will befall in your days.'[30]

From the outset of the poem, one can observe a few salient
features that both reflected and continued to shape literary
and cultural figures' approaches to politics. There are the
classic dichotomies, binary splits that were deeply embedded
in Western culture, the deepest and most important being
that of 'male' and 'female'. Rome is seen as 'female': passive,
needing a saviour from the outside, and incapable of success
on her own. The senator, on the other hand, must act actively,
powerfully, even aggressively, grabbing Rome by the hair,
shaking her awake. He is prospectively imagined as ideally
'male', in other words, in the fortunately fading (if not totally
so) model of how men were permitted to treat women. But
that set of dichotomies, framing device though it is, is only
the beginning.

As the poem goes on, Petrarch's intense mythologizing
of Rome increases in volume, as does his hope for a saviour:

> The ancient walls that the world still fears and loves
> and trembles at when it remembers past time and
> looks back; the stones where the bodies of men were
> enclosed, men who will not be without fame until the
> universe is dissolved; and everything which this one
> ruin comprehends: all hope through you to repair their
> every flaw.[31]

This valorizing of Rome – a Rome of the mind, powerful
and imperial, in stark contrast to the ruined medieval city
Petrarch had seen at first hand only a year and a half before
– is deliberate, to be placed in contrast to what Rome has
become, to what, in truth, represented the sad norm of pre-
modern life:

> And if there is any care in Heaven for earthly things,
> the souls who are citizens up there and have aban-
> doned their bodies to earth beg you for an end to the
> long civil enmity, because of which the people are not
> safe, and the path of pilgrimage to their temples is
> closed . . .[32]

To Rome's ancient, secular, imperial majesty has been added
the majesty of Christianity; nonetheless, the Eternal City finds
itself afflicted with 'civil enmity' (*odio civil*). This 'civil enmity'
was, just as in Capranica, a feature of pre-modern life in
Petrarch's Italy. Clan rivalries, kin-based social groups in competition with each other and the frequent recourse to violence
and vendetta: Rome, like other cities, was subject to these
afflictions. The fact that some of Christianity's holiest places

(churches and sacred sites in Rome where pilgrims would go) were blocked by this sort of violence only added to the sense of tension and emergency.

What does one see?

> The women in tears, the defenceless throng of the young, the exhausted old, who hate themselves and their too long life, and the black friars and the grey and the white, and all the other squadrons of the unfortunate and sick, cry out: 'O our Lord, help, help.'[33]

The problem is that Rome, a city with a long-gone ancient heritage, is bereft, torn between lawlessness and feuding nobles, seemingly without any order at all. It has potential, it has an ancient legacy, and it has possibilities. But it needs a solution for its problems.

Petrarch's solution, if one can call it that, resides not in a theory of government but in the hope that this one man, the addressee of his poem, can swoop in and resolve the problems. When it comes to effective political thinking, this sort of sentiment would not be something to take seriously, except for the fact that Petrarch, like intellectuals before him and like many after, was all too willing to support tyrannical rule in the hopes that a salvific figure who could 'fix everything' would take control.

If Petrarch's discovery of the ancient world led him to make scholarly discoveries, to write inspirational poetry and to lead the way for Italian intellectuals who came after him, there was this other side as well: that of the naive intellectual who falls under the sway of an absolute idea. In this case, the absolute idea came in the form of a person named Cola di Rienzo, as we shall see. By the time Petrarch reached that point, however, he was famous, with a reputation that spanned Europe.

THREE

A Reputation Assured

ETRARCH'S POEM *'Spirto gentil'* ('Noble Spirit') showed that he, like many, could be seduced by the promise of strong leadership in an authoritarian vein. But it signalled something else as well: that Petrarch's voice as a poet was becoming ever more authoritative and that, as he ended that one phase of his life that culminated in his trip to Rome and his visit to the Colonna household there, he was ready to begin another. It began with his return to southern France in 1337 and ended with the emergence of the Black Death in 1348. During this period, Petrarch began a series of major works in Latin, received a laurel crown, gathered together his Italian lyric poetry for the first time and befriended a tyrant.

In 1337, then, Petrarch purchased a new home in Vaucluse (which in French means 'closed valley'). Geographically, it was near the papal city of Avignon, but for Petrarch, it was worlds apart, symbolizing the power of the solitary life (illus. 12). It was here that he began almost all of his major works. This secluded place at the mouth of the river Sorgue represented a retreat of the mind as well as of the body, where the distractions and temptations of cities were far away: *linquamus urbem non redeundi animo* – 'let us leave the city behind with no

intention of returning', he wrote in one of his Latin works.[1] As he put it in his 'Letter to Posterity' regarding Vaucluse: 'This is what is essential: almost all of the works that I have happened to compose were either completed, begun or conceived there; and there were so many such works that they have continued to busy me up until this very day.'[2] Vaucluse represented one side of a twofold creative engine. The other half, as we shall see, was the need for public glory and for recognition.

Petrarch began two works during the first years of his time in Vaucluse: *On Illustrious Men* (*De viris illustribus*), a collection of lives of exemplary ancient figures, and a Latin epic poem

12 Drawing of Vaucluse, found in the margins of Petrarch's personal copy of Pliny the Elder, *Natural History*, 1350. Bottom right: 'My most joyful transalpine solitude.'

that, though it would occupy him for the rest of his life, he never fully finished. Called the *Africa*, it told the story of the Roman hero Scipio Africanus, who defeated the North African general Hannibal during the Punic Wars, after which Rome was definitively launched on its path to becoming a world power. Both works shared an interest in the exemplary nature of the ancient past: the idea that, in order to shape one's conduct in the present, one needed to look towards the past for examples of what to imitate and what to avoid.

During these years, too, Petrarch had another brush with the ancient past, this time with the practice of awarding laurel crowns to literary figures. In his 'Letter to Posterity' he tells us what happened when he was residing in Vaucluse:

> As I was living there – and it is amazing to say it! – two letters reached me on the very same day, one from the Roman senate, the other from the chancery of the University of Paris, both inviting me to receive the poetic laurel, the one suggesting I come to Rome, the other to Paris, as if they were in competition with one another.[3]

Amazing indeed. If this report sounds a little contrived, this is because it is. Petrarch had confided in his friend and confessor Dionigi da Borgo San Sepolcro, as well as to Giacomo Colonna, that he would very much appreciate it were he to receive the laurel crown. We can see echoes of these hints in the correspondence that immediately follows his letter known as the 'Ascent of Mont Ventoux'.[4] Why would Petrarch have aspired to be crowned with a laurel?

First, there was some recent history behind him. A Paduan thinker and poet named Albertino Mussato had been so crowned in his home city of Padua in 1315. And the same privilege had been offered to Dante in Bologna, though Dante refused, longing (in vain as it happened) to have that honour bestowed upon him in Florence alone.[5] Petrarch's awareness that this custom was available and that it had already happened in two cases (one fully realized) spurred him on. But there was also the symbolic importance and the idea that 'laureation' had been a custom of the ancients: literature, poetry and history could have a role in political culture. This latter point – the political one – was why Petrarch chose Rome over Paris. True, the University of Paris was, as he said in a letter to Giacomo Colonna, 'the mother of the studies of our time'. But Rome was the 'capital of the world and queen among cities', so that, in choosing Rome, the ceremony could take place over the ashes of the great ancient poets.[6]

Petrarch believed that there was one other element he needed before accepting the laurel crown: a sponsor. So he appealed to Robert of Anjou, who was the king of Naples. The hope was that the king would 'examine' Petrarch and, were Petrarch found worthy, go on to recommend Petrarch to the Roman Senate for the laurel crown. Robert had earned the nickname 'the Wise' for his support of learning, having strengthened the University of Naples and served as a patron and supporter of artists and scholars. In his 'Letter to Posterity' Petrarch described the ruler as the 'greatest king and philosopher' and as the only ruler of the time who was equally lauded 'as a friend of both wisdom and virtue'.[7]

Was there some sort of policy manual in place that speci-
fied how and under what conditions laurel crowns were to
be bestowed? No. Instead what this episode shows is that,
for all his interiority, Petrarch also had a good sense for public relations. He understood that if this king, reputed both
for his wisdom and virtue, were to tender an 'official' recommendation, Petrarch's carefully engineered crowning would
carry all the more weight. In other words, in addition to
offering Petrarch financial sponsorship, the king's backing
would give Petrarch what sociologists call 'social capital': the
strength and resources provided by a strong network of
support.

So Petrarch made his way to Naples, leaving from the port
of Marseilles in the company of another ruler he had been
cultivating (Azzo da Correggio, who would become the ruler
of Parma for four years and whom Petrarch would visit there).
Petrarch arrived in Naples, read some of his Latin epic *Africa*
to the king and was then examined over three days. When all
was said and done, the king was so enthused with Petrarch
that he wanted to present him a laurel crown in Naples. But
Petrarch was firm, he tells us in the 'Letter to Posterity', and
left Naples armed with a letter from the king, who also for
good measure sent emissaries to the Roman Senate.

A senator from a prominent Roman family, Orso dell'
Anguillara, welcomed Petrarch to a ceremony on Rome's
Capitoline Hill, one of Rome's seven hills and arguably its
most important: it was where the first Romans had placed
their citadel in the ancient world and where in the Middle
Ages the Romans placed the centre of their government.
There, Petrarch publicly read an oration he had composed

specifically for the occasion, one of the few public speeches of his that we possess.[8]

It is a curious work. Its subject was the art of poetry and, unsurprisingly for those who see Petrarch as the 'father' of Italian Renaissance humanism, it began with a quotation from Virgil: 'It is love that compels me upwards, over the lonely slopes of Parnassus' (*sed me Parnasi deserta per ardua dulcis/ raptat amor*).[9] Virgil's *Georgics*, the poetry of shepherds and flocks, of the seasons and the rhythms of nature, offers that sly allusion to Parnassus, the mountain in Greece that overlooked Delphi, Apollo's home, and was also sacred to the Muses. Petrarch's adoption of that line as his opener is telling: he is committing himself to the poetic art and also to all those other arts that the Muses represent. As the oration proceeds, however, something interesting occurs: Petrarch more or less follows the structure and techniques of a medieval sermon on holy scripture as he parses, unveils and explicates Virgil's lines.[10] On the one hand, as one scholar has eloquently put it, this approach makes of Virgil 'a classical text treated with the reverence due scripture'.[11] This sort of close, repetitive, meditative reading formed part of Petrarch's approach to much written work, secular and sacred included.

On the other hand, Petrarch's 'medieval' approach illuminates a few noteworthy facts. First, and most obviously, it shows that the tired old distinction between an idealized 'Middle Ages' and an equally idealized 'Renaissance' was much less stark than scholarship of a previous era might have proclaimed. Along these lines, Petrarch's choice in how to structure his oration shows the importance of one thing most of all: genre. Audiences have expectations, and in order to communicate effectively, it is best not to violate those expectations. The form of the sermon was familiar, its rhythms part of people's consciousness. This very familiarity of form makes the content of Petrarch's oration all the more note-worthy. It leans heavily, indeed almost exclusively, on secular ancient sources, with Cicero earning pride of place. In the ora-tion's three sections, Petrarch explains what the art of poetry is (something divinely inspired), elucidates what sort of pro-fession a poet possesses (one that instils matters that are essentially true under the veil of fiction) and, finally, asks: why now and why him?

As to that final set of queries, Petrarch suggests that it is the right moment and that he is the right person for a number of reasons. He will himself receive glory after being recog-nized with the laurel; importantly, so will those about whom he will write. Moreover, the matters to be treated, celebrated and articulated within his poetry will be useful to the city of Rome. As a means of confirming these statements, the cer-emony (which Petrarch had scripted) continued with Senator Orso reading out a citation to a gathered crowd. Among other things, he declared Petrarch a *magnus poeta et historicus* ('great poet and historian') who was to receive a laurel crown and be considered a *magister* ('master', indicating that he had the privilege to teach). Also, henceforth Petrarch would possess citizenship in Rome.[12]

What it all signified – the oration, the carefully arranged rituals, the setting – was this: Petrarch was offering up a new role for poetry and, more deeply, for the use of history and humanities scholarship in the political life of a city, and more specifically in Rome. It was a city that he had come to see from his faraway perch in France (and first only through books) as the central city in what could be a new, energized centre of power, buttressed by its monumental ancient past and energized by the return, so he hoped, of the papacy from what he often termed its 'Babylonian Captivity' in France.

But what sort of vision did Petrarch really have? How tethered to any sort of political reality was he, other than that of the classic intellectual who lobs criticisms at institutions from the outside? As mentioned, one of the works on which Petrarch had been concentrating his energies in Vaucluse, before his crowning in Rome, was the collection of biographies of exemplary ancient figures, *On Illustrious Men*. In that work's preface he says that he would have gladly written about contemporary great men, but could not, since contemporary princes 'offer material suitable not so much for history but rather for satire'.[13] This disdain for his fellow men pops up throughout Petrarch's work and career. Likely it was a manifestation of personal insecurity and intensive self-criticism that he then externalized into contempt for others. Later thinkers would take inspiration from Petrarch's thoughts on Rome and Italy, but in the day-to-day practice of politics he was hopelessly diffident, unable or unwilling to engage in the sort of tactics that enable practical politics to take place.

Perhaps this practical detachment is why, shortly after his laurel crown, he fell for Cola di Rienzo (1313–1354). Petrarch supported the unlikely ascendancy of this truly unbalanced figure, a rabble-rousing demagogue who marshalled ancient Roman symbols, persuasive political rhetoric and violence to take control, for a while, of Rome.[14] It is worth pausing with the story of Cola di Rienzo. Cola was a man of modest background, one who would have been unlikely to enter into the highly stratified ranks of public life in his day. Yet he was able to earn the title of notary, and he had three things going for him. First, he was a brilliant, self-taught student of Roman history, so that he could connect Rome's monumental, if ruined, legacy to its ancient past. Second, he possessed a gift for public speaking, a rarity at all times and an even more valuable commodity in his own era, when the sight of an orator on a street corner was not unfamiliar and when that sort of public, oral communication was at a premium, serving as a vehicle of delivering news, furthering community discussions and even providing entertainment. Third, Cola was endowed with an inborn gift for appreciating political symbols and symbolic gestures of all sorts.

His first triumph came when he was selected to serve as part of a visiting party to Avignon to meet with the pope, Clement VI. There Cola made a great impression with a rousing oration lamenting Rome's sad condition and damning the nobility, whom he termed the 'barons of Rome'. A contemporary chronicle reports Cola's indictment: 'the barons of Rome are street criminals: they consent to murder, robbery, adultery, and every form of evil. They are willing to let their city lie desolated.'[15] The pope was receptive and swayed by Cola's eloquence, but many of the Roman nobility in attendance, as well as those who heard of Cola's speech, were offended. The trip allowed his status to rise even higher than it already had, and when he returned to Rome, after almost three years of scheming and deal-making, he led an anti-noble revolt that placed him at the head of a new government. Cola took the title 'tribune of the people'. For a time, he was accepted. The nobles, for the most part, backed down, and Cola gained the confidence and esteem of the Roman people by strategically deployed symbolic acts, including public executions. Petrarch had written Cola a letter praising him and urging him on: 'Be prudent, be brave, and strength will not fail you either in protecting the liberties of the city or in reestablishing its ancient sway . . . Both God and humanity champion such a just cause.'[16]

As time went on, Cola became ever more ambitious. He believed inherently that Rome by right should have sway over all of Italy. He proposed a governing coalition based in Rome and sent letters to Italy's major rulers, urging them to send representatives to Rome for a meeting. Amazingly, at least in retrospect, a number did. Cola held this meeting and even had the audacity to presume that he could adjudicate a dispute between the Holy Roman Emperor, Louis IV, and his principal rival Charles (who soon would himself become Holy Roman Emperor under the title Charles IV).

Having returned to Rome, Cola began to levy new taxes on the Romans to support his lavish style of governance. And the people began to lose faith. Cola had a habit of seizing and imprisoning (and then usually releasing) nobles, as he did with Stefano Colonna (who by the way had been one of the leading citizens praising Petrarch publicly at his laurel crowning ceremony in 1341), and so the nobles' initial acquiescence turned into active opposition. Finally, Cola lost the pope's support, fleeing Rome and hiding out in a monastery for two years, until 1350. It was in this year that the ever more deranged Cola travelled north, to Prague, to meet in person with the emperor, now Charles IV, to attempt to persuade him to liberate Rome and Italy from the tyrannical control of the pope. To no avail. The emperor jailed Cola for a year and then delivered him to the pope himself, Clement VI, who promptly imprisoned Cola and had him tried by three cardinals, who found him guilty of numerous crimes and sentenced him to execution.

Petrarch remained a supporter through all this and wrote letters imploring Cola's release, with no result. Cola was saved only by fortune: Clement died and the new pope, Innocent VI, liked Cola's basic message regarding Rome: down with the nobles. Cola was pardoned and released and thereafter made his way back to Rome in 1354, accompanied by mercenary troops he had hired. Once again, Cola achieved a position of power in Rome, but this time his manifest lack of balance and basic sanity emerged even more quickly, as he began putting certain people to death almost arbitrarily. He soon lost the faith of the Roman people who had been eager to welcome him back. An angry crowd besieged his residence on 8 October, and though Cola tried to escape in disguise, he was soon found out, tortured mercilessly and killed.

We can see Petrarch's relationship with Cola emerging through a series of letters over the years. It is highly possible that the two knew of each other, and might have met even before some of the most noteworthy events that occurred alongside Cola's improbable rise to power. Petrarch's crowning as poet laureate in Rome in 1341 and Cola's visit to Avignon with the Roman delegation to Pope Clement VI both repre- sent times they might have met. But things really got going after Cola's victory in Rome in 1347, when Petrarch wrote a letter urging the Roman people to stand firm, to remember that they had been subjected to the tyranny of the warring nobility: 'Your liberty and the glory of your deliverer' – Petrarch means Cola di Rienzo – 'they reckon as their dishonor and disgrace'.[17] Petrarch realizes the precariousness of the current situation and the looming dangers:

> I fear there will be many, very many who, through intermarriage with the tyrants or through their long and wretched period of servitude, are persuaded that the cup of the slave is sweeter than the abstinence of the freeman. There will be many who believe that they have attained a great and noble end if they are greeted on the streets or are summoned hastily by their lords and plagued by lewd commands. There will be many famished filthy parasites who seat themselves at their tyrant's wicked table and greedily gulp down whatever escapes their lords' gullets.[18]

So what, really, did Petrarch fear? He feared precisely the fundamental, grounding conditions of the Italy in which he lived, where family connections ('intermarriage') were more important than merit, where public recognition was quite important ('greeted on the streets'), and where reciprocal favours underlay most important relationships ('gulp down whatever escapes . . .').

In other words, one side of Petrarch feared what he recognized to be true: that the conditions of life then were conducive to things slipping back into the way they were previously. We would recognize these conditions as embodying, more or less, the basic principles of a face-to-face pre-modern society: local, kin-based and ruled by rituals of recognition.

Petrarch could only counterpose an imagined lost world of 'liberty', the world he would have conjured, as would so many, from Livy's idealized presentation in his *History*, of virtuous, simple Romans, who fought their own wars, governed themselves and gave rise to an empire; an empire such as Rome might produce again, if only the conditions were right – if only the right leader emerged.

So when Petrarch shifts the addressee from the Roman people to Cola, the transition is dramatic: 'But you, most brave man, you who have buttressed the immense weight of the tottering state with your patriotic shoulders, gird yourself and watch with equal vigilance against such citizens as against the most bitter enemy.'[19] Petrarch casts Cola as the saviour, indeed as a saviour in a particular mould: 'You, younger Brutus, always keep the example of the first Brutus before you.'[20] This was the Brutus who had thrown off the rule of the Tarquins in Rome's earliest history, as Livy had recorded Rome's transition from a monarchy early on to a republic. With his reminiscence here, Petrarch wants to inspire Cola to fulfil that same role in select ways. Most importantly: 'do not heed considerations of either birth or affection.'[21]

From strategies of rule, Petrarch moves to exhortation and an appeal to the past. He asks:

> What inspiration, in truth, is not to be derived from the memory of the past and from the grandeur of a name once revered throughout the world? Who does not wish Rome the best of fortune in her endeavors to attain her rightful empire? Both God and humanity champion such a just cause.[22]

The past serves as inspiration to dream, and Petrarch reveals the dream, or at least its trajectory, in the next sentence: 'Italy, which only recently lay listless and enfeebled, with head bowed to the ground, has now risen to her knees.'[23] This is the dream: that 'Italy', here envisioned as a sleeping colossus, will rise once more.

Petrarch's letter to Cola goes on in this vein, as Petrarch recalls ancient Roman examples, urges Cola to read accounts of ancient Roman history and, finally, changes his addressee once more, with direct address to the Roman citizenry: 'But you, O citizens, now for the first time truly deserving the name of citizens, be fully convinced that this man has been sent to you from heaven.'[24] Petrarch encourages the Romans to remember how often they have spilled their own blood and lost their own resources only to help the irresponsible nobility in their seemingly endless quest for unlimited power. Just as the virtuous ancient Romans threw off the kings of old and established the Roman republic, so too should pres- ent-day Romans, with Cola di Rienzo as their leader, throw off the yoke of the local, rapacious, war-like nobility and reclaim their ancient legacy: liberty, 'liberty for which men have rid Rome of its kings and have deprived the Caesars of their lives'.[25]

By 'liberty' Petrarch means here, more or less, freedom from outside rule and, in this limited Roman case, freedom from grasping local nobility imposing their will without the consent of the governed. That, however, is about as far as it goes. He is not proposing democratic institutions that would be recognizable to modern eyes. His conception is largely negative and rhetorical: negative, in the sense that he sees (as did many in his day) what a city should not look like (dominated by a few powerful local families with no concern for the citizenry); rhetorical, in the sense that his appeal, both to the Roman people and to Cola di Rienzo, is emotional, rooted in a desire to use ancient examples – chosen in a very particular way – to move the spirits of his audience. It is, finally, their common interest that should unite them: 'Cling to each other tenaciously, peaceably.'[26]

Petrarch's letter foreshadows much of what was important about Italian Renaissance intellectual life, as well as pointing towards some of the blind spots to which Renaissance thinkers succumbed. On the positive side: a strong sense of history and a passion for the ancient world led to framing arguments that could have a direct relevance for contemporary life. On the negative side: a selective reading of ancient history and a distance from the give and take of real politics could serve to evince an unrealistic idealism that in practice could never be fulfilled, not to mention a dangerous faith in the potential of salvific leaders – in that one imaginary person who by personal virtue could lead a whole society from sickness into health. Petrarch came to regret his early faith in Cola, as Cola's lack of basic sanity emerged with clarity. But the hope and the need for strong rulers would define the political experience of Italy's city-states in the Renaissance, without ever leading to that mythical status – a unified Italian nation – towards which Petrarch pointed, if inchoately.

Petrarch's legacy, like that of almost all Renaissance intellectuals, rests not with his political views but with his work both creative and scholarly, work that set the tone for the five generations to follow. By far the work for which he best known today is his *Canzoniere*, the collection of Italian poems that included '*Spirto gentil*', which we have examined above. Yet – to circle back for a moment to his laureation on Rome's Capitoline Hill, where he was crowned as 'great poet and historian' – it is worth mentioning that it was only about two years *after* that ceremony that he began seriously to gather together the various Italian poems that made up the *Canzoniere*. As is the case for almost all of his works, Petrarch continued working on the *Canzoniere* his whole life. The version we now have includes 366 poems, most of which are in sonnet form (illus. 13). The different titles by which this collection is known reveal much. *Canzoniere* means simply a 'collection of songs', and is as such the most neutral title (the equation 'song=poem' had ancient roots, and referred to the fact that poems would be recited, often in a sing-song and rhythmic way). Petrarch also referred to this collection as *Rime sparse*, an Italian expression that means 'scattered rhymes'. Finally, he referred to it also with a Latin title: *Rerum vulgarium fragmenta*, 'fragments of things in the vernacular', literally understood.

These titles point to the paradox that shapes our understanding of Petrarch: he deliberately downplayed his vernacular work, at least overtly, depicting his meticulously crafted poems as 'scattered' and as 'fragments'. It was his Latin work that he saw as lasting (and deserving of the laurel crown), whereas he presented his vernacular poetry as a series of trifles. But this paradox exists only on the surface. Petrarch never stopped working on his poems: he continued to reorder them throughout his life, even as he put a great deal of emotion into their crafting. Take the first poem:

13 The first page from a Venetian manuscript of *Il Canzoniere* from 1400, with illuminations attributed to Cristoforo Cortese (1390–1445).

Voi ch'ascoltate in rime sparse il suono
   di quei sospiri ond'io nudriva 'l core
     in sul mio primo giovenile errore quand'era in parte altr'uom
da quel ch'i'sono: del vario stile in ch'io piango et ragiono,
   fra le vane speranze e 'l van dolore, ove sia chi per prova
intenda amore, spero trovar pietà, nonché perdono.
   Ma ben veggio or sì come al popol tutto favola fui gran
tempo, onde sovente di me medesmo meco mi vergogno;
   et del mio vaneggiar vergogna è il frutto, e 'l pentersi, e 'l
conoscer chiaramente che quanto piace al mondo è breve sogno.[27]

You who hear in scattered rhymes the sound of those sighs with which I nourished my heart during my first youthful error, when I was in part another man from what I am now: for the varied style in which I weep and speak between vain hopes and vain sorrow, where there is anyone who understands love through experience, I hope to find pity, not only pardon. But now I see well how for a long time I was the talk of the crowd, for which often I am ashamed of myself within: and of my raving, shame is the fruit, and repentance, and the clear knowledge that whatever pleases in the world is a brief dream.[28]

Petrarch's wording sets the tone for the whole collection.

The first line foregrounds the 'scattered rhymes' and thus sets forth the author's desired self-image of humility. Next, he speaks of the 'sighs' of his 'youthful error'. 'Error' – the Italian *errore* – could just as easily be translated as 'wandering'. The implication is that the poet spent his youth on a wandering path, and that he can now look back, having set himself straight. There is self-consciousness regarding style ('varied style'), and there is the deliberate presentation of self as an emotionally involved, intensely self-aware person ('I weep'). He seeks 'pity' – 'compassion', really – and realizes as ever that his fame was great ('I was the talk of the crowd') and that his 'raving' (the Italian word is *vaneggiar*, which can also mean 'boasting') has engendered within himself shame and a desire to repent, since 'whatever pleases in the world is a brief dream.'

All of Petrarch's contradictions emerge in this brief poem: the need to discuss his vernacular poetry combined with the need to downplay its significance, to vaunt his fame while simultaneously minimizing its importance, to view his earlier love interests as the centre of his affective self while seeing them, hauntingly, as a phase that needed to be surpassed. This first poem introduces the collection and was finished well after many of the other poems were written (during his lifetime Petrarch collected, arranged and reordered the poems in the *Canzoniere* nine different times). Their subject, overwhelmingly, is indeed Petrarch's early 'love', if it can be called that, for Laura, the woman he idolized from afar after seeing her at Mass on 6 April 1327. Or maybe we should say the woman he 'may have seen'. We know nothing, in truth, about Laura as a person, though some scholars have made attempts to identify her.[29]

The date of 6 April 1327 comes to us from two sources. The first is a note that Petrarch wrote in 1348 in the flyleaf of the 'Ambrosian Virgil', as we have seen. In that note, Petrarch relates that he has just heard from a friend that Laura passed away: 'the light of her life', he writes, 'was subtracted from the light of day, while I, alas, was at Verona, unknowing of my fate'.[30] Some scholars have even suggested that Petrarch wrote the note later, in 1351, but back-dated it to 1348, since the number seven held significance for him and he could thus mark three seven-year periods in which he had known her. It is fair to say that Laura, for him, whether he actually knew her personally or not, came to represent a faraway object of desire and longing, a muse whose luminous presence in his mind inspired the *Canzoniere*.

This sense can be observed in the second of the two sources that indicate the date Petrarch first saw Laura, the poem in the *Canzoniere* entitled '*Voglia mi sprona*' – 'Desire Spurs Me', which we have encountered earlier:

> *Voglia mi sprona, Amor mi guida et scorge, Piacer mi tira,*
> *Usanza mi trasporta; Speranza mi lusinga et riconforta et la man*
> *destra al cor già stanco porge,*
>
> > *e 'l misero la prende et non s'accorge di nostra cieca e disleale*
> > *scorta; regnano i sensi et la ragion è morta; de l'un vago desio l'al-*
> > *tro risorge.*
>
> > *Vertute, onor, bellezza, atto gentile, dolci parole ai bei rami*
> > *m'han giunto ove soavemente il cor s'invesca.*
>
> > *Mille trecento ventisette, a punto su l'ora prima, il dí sesto*
> > *d'aprile, nel laberinto intrai, né veggio ond'esca.*[31]

Desire spurs me, Love guides and escorts me, Pleasure draws me, Habit carries me away; Hope entices and encourages me and reaches out his right hand to my weary heart, and my wretched heart grasps it and does not see how blind and treacherous this guide of ours is; the senses govern and reason is dead; and one yearning desire is born after another. Virtue, honor, beauty, gentle bearing, sweet words brought us to the lovely branches, that my heart may be sweetly enlimed. One thousand three hundred twenty-seven, exactly at the first hour of the sixth day of April, I entered the labyrinth, nor do I see where I may get out of it.[32]

'Love' – by which Petrarch means the god of love, Cupid, by whose arrow he had been struck so long ago – is his guide, but Love is a 'blind' guide, one who is 'treacherous'. The treachery leads to one desire being born after another, in a perpetually unsatisfying cycle, wherein Petrarch is trapped (as if in a 'labyrinth'), condemned to see what he cannot touch, desire what he cannot have and live in a tormented state of unfulfilment. It was 'virtue, honor, beauty, gentle bearing, sweet words' that brought him to the tree, like an unsuspecting bird who, seeking only a seemingly natural place to alight, is trapped in resin ('enlimed').

As Petrarch tells us, towards the end of the poem, the date when his love for Laura began (carefully crafted, yet again, for he believed that the date, 6 April, was the same as Christ's crucifixion), we realize that this poem, like his love for Laura as manifested so hauntingly in the *Canzoniere*, is an allegory. His desire for the unreachable Laura, spurred on by Cupid's arrows, seems a lot like the central mystery of Christian life, as Petrarch would have understood it: our life is driven forward by a mysterious force, one with which we will only be united after our death. Petrarch's love for Laura epitomizes this earthly struggle, so that his poetry transcends normal love poetry and reaches a much higher level.

The *Canzoniere* also enters on occasion into politics, as we have seen in the case of the poem '*Spirto gentil*' and as we can see ever more strongly in the poem '*Italia mia*' – 'My Italy'. Petrarch wrote this poem during his lengthy period of infatuation with Cola di Rienzo, and it contains some themes that will by now ring familiar. Recall that Petrarch had travelled from France to Naples in the company of Azzo da Correggio, a northern Italian military captain (or *condottiero* in Italian), who was interested in taking control of the city of Parma, which is near Milan. In 1340, with Petrarch beside him, Azzo married into a noble family of that region, the Gonzaga, and soon thereafter he conquered his desired city. Petrarch went to visit him there and stayed a while, eventually being caught in the crossfire (metaphorically speaking) of a military battle between Azzo and a member of another branch of the very Gonzaga family into which he had married, an extended episode that occurred in the years 1344–5. It is to this period that '*Italia mia*' dates. Though there are clearly references in the poem that refer to the situation of Parma and the ongoing battles there, the poem transcended its immediate context and became a touchstone for outbreaks of Italian national feeling, so much so that Machiavelli would quote it as the final lines of his famous *The Prince* over one hundred and fifty years later.

The poem begins in a passionately plaintive fashion, with a direct address to Italy: 'My Italy, it is true that speaking will address only in vain the mortal wounds that I see covering your body so densely. Still I'd like my sighing words to give hope to the Tiber, the Arno, and the Po, where I sit now, so gravely grieving.'[33] Already Petrarch has signalled much. The three rivers offer a geography: the Tiber is Rome's great river,

the Arno that of Tuscany and Florence more specifically, and
the Po that of Milan, near where Petrarch sits, in distress at
the 'mortal wounds' that are tearing Italy apart.

Thereafter he invokes God – *Rettor del cielo* – 'ruler of
heaven' – and asks Him to cast his gaze down upon a place
(Italy, implicitly) where 'such cruel war has arisen from such
trivial causes'.[34] Petrarch then asserts his right to be heard as
a poet and his hope that his poem will have an effect: 'And
the hearts that proud, savage Mars has hardened and locked
up: may you open them, Father, and soften them and loose
their knots. There let your truth be sung through my lips,
howsoever small I may be.'[35] As in the case of his '*Spirto gentil*',
addressed to a Roman senator, Petrarch has a sincere belief
that poetry can influence the world of politics and war.

Having dealt with God, he now turns to Italy's rulers: 'You
to whom Fortune has entrusted rule over our fine regions, for
which it seems you feel no pity: what are so many foreign
swords doing here?'[36] 'Foreign swords': *pellegrine spade* is the Italian Petrarch uses. *Spade* – 'swords' – is straightforward. *Pellegrine*
– 'foreign' – carries with it also the meanings in its Latin root,
peregrinus, which can signify a traveller or even a pilgrim. The
result is that, while Petrarch is indeed pointing first and foremost to the presence of groups he wishes to designate as
'foreigners', there is also an implied lament that Italy, the
land where pilgrims travel, lacks any sort of cohesiveness, and
that those who come from without (so says Petrarch, who
grew up in France) prove destructive to Italy's well-being
and potential flourishing. He likens the foreigners to a flood,
one whose destructive presence on Italian soil is due to the
weakness of Italy's ruling class.

What he is talking about, in case it is unclear to a modern reader, is the use of mercenary soldiers, whom the rulers (or would-be rulers) of Italian city-states routinely employed to supplement their own forces in their constant military adventures. But Petrarch says, still addressing these feckless rulers, that they are flattering themselves with a 'vain error', as they 'look for love, or good faith, in venal hearts'.[37] The complaint, in short, is that these soldiers are fighting for nothing other than pay and have no reason to be loyal to you, if you are a ruler, other than that. It is a complaint that, after Petrarch, would be heard on and off in Italy until, in the early sixteenth century, Machiavelli devoted a whole chapter to the problem in his *The Prince*, evincing the same basic idea: Italian rulers don't know how to rule and are all too willing to outsource basic military matters to people who have no inherent motivation to carry out their responsibilities.

Petrarch's next move in '*Italia mia*' is to suggest that Italy possesses a natural border to the north in the form of the Alps: 'Nature provided well for our estate, when it set up the Alps as a shield between us and the rabid Germans.'[38] He then circles back, heaping further reprobation on the German mercenary soldiers and their 'Bavarian trickery' as, instead of fighting, they 'raise their fingers and play games with death' – meaning, instead of battling as they are supposed to do, they signal each other to take it easy instead of fighting until death.[39]

Petrarch reminds the unnamed rulers of Italy (to whom '*Italia mia*' is addressed) that they possess 'noble Latin blood' and as such should be ashamed to let Germans or any other foreigners get the better of them. And then, Petrarch injects himself back into his poetic address, when he asks, regarding

Italy: 'Is this not the ground I first touched? The nest where I was so sweetly nurtured? Is this not the homeland, a sweet pious mother, in which I place all my faith and where both my parents now rest?'[40] The poet is relying on his own presence to persuade hard-bitten politicians that they must change the way they think about governance and about the primacy of a strong home-grown military. If they do – and here are the poem's most famous lines, with which Machiavelli much later ended *The Prince* – 'Virtue will take up arms against rage and the fighting will be short, since the ancient strength in Italian hearts is not yet dead.'[41]

Most prominent is the way Petrarch links ancient with modern virtue – or better, with the potential of realizing virtue in his own era. As he reaches for models of political and military behaviour, he skips over anything we would recognize as the Middle Ages, a tendency consistent with his work elsewhere. For although he did see certain leading figures, King Robert of Naples among them, as possessing virtue, Petrarch's general view of his contemporaries and of Italy's leadership class was low. In many respects, in this poem and in much of his other writing, he forcefully inaugurates a tendency that will last throughout the Italian Renaissance: looking towards antiquity to teach virtuous political conduct to contemporary political and military elites.[42] What has sometimes puzzled scholars of political theory is that these sorts of recommendations don't always, or even often, occur in works that seem on the surface to be works of political theory. Instead, these counsels tend to be subtle, located in poems (as here), or in dialogues, letters, histories and other sorts of treatises. Here the implied virtue is self-reliance for Italy's city-states, something they cannot achieve without having rulers who by their own exemplary conduct allow that strength to flourish. It is a strength that perhaps, Petrarch believed, only existed in potential, but that could be brought to actuality if Italy's leaders stopped bringing foreign soldiers in to fight battles they should be attending to themselves.

Here as in the case of Petrarch's infatuation with Cola di Rienzo, it is important to note that the language of exhortation – ever appealing and always easy to listen to – sits uneasily next to a lack of realism and an inability to perceive the on-the-ground conditions under which Italy's city-states were operating. Their small size, their endemic family- and kin-based violence and the lack of common political habits among them: these and other factors meant that calls for Italian unity almost always came from people who either had a vantage point beyond the peninsula, like Petrarch, or who were in exile from their own cities, as Dante had been – who also at times pointed towards the need for Italian unity.

Petrarch concludes '*Italia mia*' by speaking directly to his poem:

> Song, let me advise you to proclaim your message in a courtly fashion, since you'll need to travel among people who are proud, whose wills are already formed by bad habits acquired long ago, habits that are always the enemy of the truth. You will find success among those few whose souls are great, whom good conduct pleases. Say to them: 'who will keep me safe? I call out as I go: Peace, Peace, Peace.'[43]

Petrarch's psychological ploy of persuasion is obvious. Those who hear this poem, those who agree with and absorb its message, will be able to count themselves among the great-souled men of the present, few though these are. It will be from among them that real leaders will rise, a select few capable of leading Italy forwards by looking backwards to its time of greatest glory, even as they accept and protect what is most beneficial and distinctive about the modern world: Christianity, which Petrarch sees as a key ingredient, along with ancient Roman virtue, in any potential contemporary success.

As he wrote this poem, Petrarch was also engaged in his correspondence with Cola di Rienzo. From that correspondence, from Petrarch's laurel crown ceremony and from 'Italia mia', we can see that, among other things, Petrarch was famous by the mid-1340s, a voice in the culture of his day and someone who could at least be assured a hearing among contemporary political leaders. His reputation, in other words, was assured by that point.

He was also a middle-aged man. In 1344 he passed the age of forty and what the ancients would have called his *acme*, the high point of flourishing. By this point he had already had a son, named Giovanni, who by 1344 was seven years old, as well as a daughter, Francesca, born in 1343. For all Petrarch's idealization of Laura, he never recorded the name of the women who bore him his children; nor did he speak much about the children themselves. In the flyleaf of the 'Ambrosian Virgil', where he recorded the deaths of those close to him, Petrarch wrote the following upon his son Giovanni's death in 1361:

Our Giovanni, a man born to hardship and to my tribulation, one who when alive vexed me with serious and
never-ending cares and who, when he died, wounded
me with bitter tribulation, died in the Year of Our
Lord 1361, at the age of 25, on the tenth day of July . . .
The news came to me at Padua on the fourteenth of the
month during vespers. He died at Milan in that publicly ruinous though unusual outbreak of plague, one
that found and then fell upon that city, which up to
that point had been immune to such evils.[44]

Children, plague, death: if one side of Petrarch's life and
thought was public, engaged with political leaders and craving
recognition in public fora, another was radically private, driv-
ing his focus and intellectual energies in upon himself and on
his own delicate psyche. His physical desires (the outcomes of
which were the children whose mothers he never named), the
precariousness of human life and his final decision to move to
Italy for good: these and more spurred Petrarch's inner life,
to which we now turn.

FOUR

The Interior Man

HE YEAR 1347 SAW PETRARCH thinking about what we would today call 'life choices'. He visited his beloved brother, Gherardo, who, four years previously, had gone to live in community with the Carthusian monks at Montrieux.[1] Questions arose. What sort of life was best? A life in the world, engaged in politics and in search of glory for literary works? Or a life of retreat from the world – the monastic ideal that Gherardo had chosen, a style of life where one could contemplate, practise one's Christian faith and leave behind all of the outside world's temptations? Petrarch was not the first, nor would he be the last, to think about the differences between the active and contemplative life. But he experienced that tension as viscerally as any other thinker before or since. It suffuses almost all of his work.

Take, for just one instance, his treatise *On Religious Leisure*. Petrarch began it in 1347 and worked on it for several years. The treatise is written in the form of a long letter with different short sections. Overall, we see Petrarch trying on a persona: that of the pious and meditative thinker. He had been tremendously impressed by his visit to the monastery, he suggests: 'I came into paradise; I saw the angels of God living on earth and in earthly bodies, destined to live in heaven and come to

Christ . . .'² Having returned from his visit, he wanted to write before the powerful impressions with which he had been left could dissipate. At the outset he tells his addressee what his stylistic aim is to be: 'I shall control my pen so that my letter to those who are distant may be for me something like a conversation with those who are present, although (to confess the truth) I may be present only in both the nobler and better part of myself.'³ The tone is to be conversational, even if Petrarch is well aware that not all sides of his complicated personality will emerge.

Petrarch's main impulse in the treatise is to offer gentle counsel to the monks, shaped by sources from Scripture and the Christian tradition, but most of all by the spirit of St Augustine (354–430 CE). This venerable thinker, traditionally considered one of the four Latin Fathers of the Church (alongside saints Jerome, Ambrose and Gregory the Great), offered a powerful vision of the human condition at the twilight of the Roman Empire. Above all St Augustine stressed the omnipotence and omniscience of God, drawing out the consequences of that view when contemplating humanity. If God is infinite and infinitely powerful, on the one hand, and human beings, His creations, are finite, on the other, then this human world we inhabit can only be a way station, a pilgrimage whose temporary pains and pleasures will be resolved in the afterlife, where matters eternal reside. Petrarch internalized these messages deeply.

In one telling part of *On Religious Leisure*, for example, Petrarch writes about how delicate the human condition is, how subject to disaster and misfortune. Petrarch goes through ancient calamities well known from his historical studies, touches on the invasions that ended the Roman Empire, and even comments on contemporary events, such as 'the plague, which without precedent is mowing down the whole mortal race from the rising to the setting of the sun as if it carried a sickle'.[4] He goes on to list the series of woes, afflictions and types of suffering to which human beings are subject, from illness, to neediness, to, finally, 'humanity's sins, which have created all the problems and the remaining plagues of the world, which are innumerable and limitless'.[5] It is only in this fashion that one can comprehend the majesty of God: by realizing the immense distance that separates Him (infinite, infinitely good, infinitely powerful) from humanity (finite, subject to countless afflictions and sinful). 'Who could explain in human words, or even conceive in the human mind, the magnitude of His grace or the height of His counsel for the sons of humanity?'[6] Petrarch counsels the monks (and by implication all of his readers) that the gulf between humanity and divinity is immense: 'Horror and astonishment strike the mind of the person who contemplates both our own low estate and God's height at the same time.'[7] For all those who connect the Renaissance with a positive image of humanity's potential, statements like this should prove how diverse Renaissance thought was, how it went through phases, and how it had protagonists with vastly differing outlooks.

On Religious Leisure has much more in it, of course, than the rather stark content of this chapter implies. There is advice on how to avoid the temptations of wealth and power, how to subdue the desires of the flesh and how to comply with the demands of the monastic life, all buttressed by countless allusions to, and citations of, scripture. Petrarch ends by asking the monks to pray for him. The treatise, though in form a letter, becomes a meditation, a kind of conversation (as Petrarch had urged) and a set piece on how to read and interpret, so that extensive citation from different sources emerges as a significant method for creating positive advice.

The reference to 'the plague' occurred almost in passing in *On Religious Leisure*. Yet it calls out for comment, since it was one of the most momentous events to occur in Petrarch's lifetime and one that affected him greatly, as it did so many others. In Western Europe the Black Death occurred from 1346–53, and, all told, killed anywhere from 30 to 60 per cent of the population.[8] And it should be added: that figure veered towards the high end for much of Italy. There have been divergent scholarly explanations for how the plague spread and whence it derived. The most commonly accepted theory is that a noxious bacillus (called 'yersinia pestis' and leading to bubonic plague) was borne by rats on commercial ships that followed trade routes from east to west. While many connected the course of the plague with ships, the germ theory of disease was centuries away, and the role of the rats went all but unnoticed. Not that it would have mattered all that much, as fourteenth-century medicine was far from being able to deal with the disease.

To understand the contemporary impact of the Black Death, we can turn to the most famous description of it that exists, by none other than Giovanni Boccaccio, who became one of Petrarch's very best friends. Boccaccio begins his otherwise humorous *Decameron* (a set of one hundred stories in the vernacular) with a lengthy description of the plague's arrival and effects in the city of Florence:

whether it descended on us mortals through the
influence of the heavenly bodies or was sent down by
God in His righteous anger to chastise us because of
our wickedness, it had begun some years before in
the East, where it deprived countless beings of their
lives before it headed to the West, spreading ever-
greater misery as it moved relentlessly from place to
place. Against it all human wisdom and foresight were
useless.[9]

Boccaccio describes the inefficacy of all efforts, be they in the
realm of public sanitation or prayer, against the plague; his
descriptions of the plague's symptoms are as harrowing as
they are disgusting: 'in men and women alike, certain swellings
would develop in the groin or under the armpits, some of
which would grow like an ordinary apple and others like an
egg, some larger and some smaller.'[10] Soon people also began
to develop spots on their bodies, a sure sign of impending
death. Medicine and the advice of doctors were useless, according to Boccaccio, 'and since none of them had any idea what
was causing the disease, they could hardly prescribe an appropriate remedy for it'. And so, 'in almost every case, death
occurred within three days after the appearance of the signs
we have described.'[11]

But the biggest problem of all was that the plague was
spread by contact between people, 'just as a fire will catch
dry or oily materials when they are placed right beside it'.[12]
Boccaccio goes on to tell of startling disturbances to the social
order as people ceased to follow their usual customs, their
routines and rituals having been disturbed by the advent of

the plague. Some people, Boccaccio relates, believed that living abstemiously would allow them to resist the plague, so they gathered in small groups and isolated themselves from the normal rhythms of society. They would, effectively, lock themselves inside with their own set-aside food and wine, speaking to no one from outside, 'nor did they want to hear news about the dead and the dying, and instead, they passed their time playing music and enjoying whatever other amusements they could devise'.[13] Others went in the opposite direction from moderation, drinking heavily, singing and laughing at everything and gathering in taverns or private homes with like-minded revellers. Boccaccio says: 'Such places were easy to find, because people, feeling that their days were numbered, not just abandoned themselves but all their possessions, too.'[14] The normal rules of possession and property seemed suspended, as homes started to be shared in common. These people too avoided all contact with those who were ill. Respect for law 'both divine and human' diminished to the point of disappearing. Other people held fine herbs and flowers to their noses, believing that these odours might help protect them from the disease, and other still fled the city, leaving behind 'their homes, their relatives, their properties and possessions, and headed for the countryside'.[15] It was as if they thought that God's wrath was directed not so much at people but at the city of Florence itself, or perhaps 'they simply concluded that no one in Florence would survive and that the city's last hour had come.'[16]

Reactions to the plague, in other words, were all over the map. Beyond the horrifying symptoms and people's diverse reactions, what seems to have affected Boccaccio most deeply was the way in which the normal patterns of close-knit family and kin relations were disturbed (illus. 14). Not only did fellow citizens avoid one another (which was bad enough), but

> the tribulation of the plague had put such fear into the hearts of men and women that brothers abandoned brothers, uncles their nephews, sisters their brothers, and very often wives their husbands . . . Fathers and mothers refused to tend to their children and take care of them, treating them as if they belonged to someone else.[17]

When all was said and done, there was not enough consecrated ground available to bury the vast quantities of the dead, the countryside was equally affected and, within the city walls, 'more than one hundred thousand human beings were deprived of their lives'.[18] That last figure is exaggerated for rhetorical effect (a common practice in pre-modern writing). But it is not that exaggerated. For Florence, recent scholarly estimates have suggested a death rate of approximately 60 per cent, which would put the actual number anywhere from 50,000 to 80,000.[19] It would be difficult to overstate the sort of psychological trauma that individuals (and society at large) would experience even today with death rates that high. In a pre-modern era, when modern medicine did not exist, the effects were wide-ranging. Boccaccio's description, for all its literary art, is penetratingly accurate. It is worth emphasizing, as well, that the Renaissance in many ways represents a world constructed by survivors of a societally traumatic event.

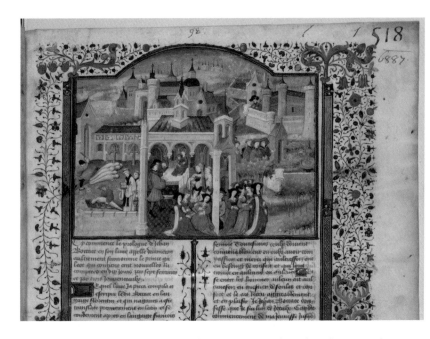

To return to Petrarch, we can say that the plague and its associated anxieties manifested themselves in various ways and, moreover, had the effect of intensifying certain tendencies in his personality. First, he knew people who died. Most meaningfully, there was the case of Laura, about whose demise he wrote in one of his death notes in the 'Ambrosian Virgil'. It is one of the lengthiest such notes in the manuscript, and it is suggestive. He begins by saying: 'Laura, famous for her own virtues and long celebrated in my poetry, first appeared to my eyes in the time of my early youth . . .'.[20] He gives the year and day (6 April 1327, as he had it in his poem '*Voglia mi sprona*') and then moves to her death, saying that she died on the very same day of the month, news of which reached him in May in a letter from a friend. Petrarch then

14 Manuscript illumination depicting the plague in Florence from a 1414 French edition of Giovanni Boccaccio's *Decameron*, translated by Laurent de Premierfait.

tells where her body ('most chaste, most beautiful') was buried (in Avignon), and he ends his death notice in a manner that is worth highlighting, suggesting as he does that there might very well have been one good thing to come out of all this. Petrarch relates that, 'now that these fetters have been broken, I am forcibly reminded of this fact: that it is time to flee Babylon, given how fast time is passing and how very fleeting in my age.'[21] In other words, he is writing (to himself, in his own copy of Virgil, in a note that he cannot have intended many others to see) that a moment has arisen where he must think seriously about doing something about which he has been dreaming for quite some time. He must leave Avignon, or 'Babylon' (in his denigrating reference that refers to the ancient Persian city's reputation as the place of the tower of Babel and as a city that rebelled against God); and he must move, finally and irrevocably, to Italy.[22] Even Laura's death, in one respect at least, is all about Petrarch and his inner struggles.

And yet, every time one finds one of these egoistic episodes in Petrarch's life, one then comes up against another counter-tendency that bespeaks sincerity and real inner turmoil. Around the same time as the plague hit and concomitant with Laura's death, Petrarch was working on a book in dialogue form called *On the Secret Conflict of My Cares*, or *The Secret* for short. Petrarch began this work in 1347, soon after his visit to his brother Gherardo at the Carthusian monastery (and thus when the contemplative life and its appeals were weighing heavily on his mind). He worked on it through 1353, when the plague had come and gone. During that period, too, he actually did what his death notice to Laura suggested: he decided definitively to leave Avignon for Italy. In one of his letters to Cola di Rienzo, Petrarch had written that 'things will go according to the manner in which eternal law has decided. I cannot change these things, but I can flee them.'[23] Petrarch, as one scholar has rightly emphasized, was a traveller, and his itinerancy emerged for numerous reasons: from his early years, where it was forced upon him, to his search for antiquity's gravity in Rome, to his endless search for patronage throughout the rest of his life.[24] But there was another kind of travel, a travel within the mind, one that grew out of what we can term a 'dialogical' sensibility.

A dialogue, strictly speaking, is a literary work in which two or more interlocutors are present, whose conversations complement and sometimes contrast with one another. Since Graeco-Roman antiquity, there have been many different types of dialogues. Those of Plato are probably the most famous among ancient dialogues. Many had Socrates, Plato's teacher, as the principal interlocutor, as Plato's mouthpiece on occasion and more usually to serve as the voice of reason who, through what would later be called Socratic questioning, would elicit the truth from the other interlocutor. Other models surfaced in antiquity and the Middle Ages. Cicero offered dialogues with larger numbers of speakers than those of Plato, in the hope of presenting different philosophical positions: one speaker would expound on one philosophical school, one on another, and so on. Though most of Plato's and some of Cicero's dialogues were lost to the Middle Ages, a great variety of dialogues developed in the medieval period.

What is striking – and what exemplifies the potential of the dialogue form – is that different positions all get an airing, and that there is not a heavy authorial presence telling the reader which one is correct. In truth, even if there were, the brilliance of the dialogue form is that, structured conversationally as dialogues are, the reader in a sense becomes another interlocutor, so that the positions can inform what the reader thinks, even as he or she is not straight-jacketed into agreeing with one or the other. It was this type of approach that many Italian intellectuals from Petrarch onwards took on board from the long dialogical tradition: using reasoning not only to solve questions but to stimulate them.

So it was meaningful that Petrarch turned to this form when he wrote his *Secret* and equally noteworthy that he did not circulate the *Secret* during his lifetime, as he did with many other works, complete or incomplete. Petrarch seems truly to have considered this work as something for himself alone, a kind of spiritual aid, one in which the dialogic back and forth represented as much a way of life as it did a formal technique of composition. As he wrote in the preface to the *Secret*, addressing the book itself, 'therefore you, O little book, fleeing from the gatherings of men, will be content to remain with me.'[25] The *Secret* is structured on the model of a Socratic dialogue, with the two characters being 'Franciscus', a version of Petrarch himself, and 'Augustinus', a version of one of Petrarch's models, St Augustine. And there was one crucial addition: a silent character, Lady Truth, who is assigned a place of observance, watching over the conversation. She appeared to Petrarch while he was deep in thought, he writes, a radiant woman who 'seemed, by her carriage and face, to be a virgin'. She thus serves as a kind of guarantee – to Petrarch as a writer and eventual reader of his own work and to other eventual, possible readers – that he was baring his soul in an honest fashion.

The issue at hand in the dialogue is Petrarch's uncertainty about a conflict that rages within himself, a conflict between that to which he is drawn by his nature (love and glory) and that to which he believes he must, as a Christian, incline: contemplation and a rejection of both physical love and the prideful seductions of literary glory.

The most important element of the dialogue is the presence of St Augustine, who had himself wrestled with some of these very same issues. Perhaps the most famous of the Latin church fathers, Augustine authored two of the medieval Western world's most important books, the *Confessions* and the *City of God*. The *Confessions*, on one hand, presented the archetypal story of conversion. Augustine told the story of how, as a youth born in North Africa to a mother who was a Christian, he matured into a pagan young adult, loving the pleasures of the world and engaging in 'the sins of the flesh that polluted my soul'.[26] Addicted to lust, he could hear the 'clank of my chains'. It was only when he submitted to the Lord that he was saved. As Augustine told the story, he was ready to become a fully fledged Christian, even as he continued to be wracked with doubt. Then, once, when he was in Milan, in the year 386 (by our current reckoning), he heard a child's voice in a garden, saying, in Latin, *tolle, lege*: 'take and read'. He opened a Bible that he had in hand to the first passage that presented itself, and he came upon Paul's 'Letter to the Romans'. There Augustine read a passage that included these words: 'let us conduct ourselves becomingly as in the day, not in reveling and drunkenness, not in debauchery and licentiousness, not in quarreling and jealousy. But put on the Lord Jesus Christ, and make no provision for the flesh, to gratify its desires.'[27] Immediately upon reading that passage, he felt his heart become flooded with light as doubt was dispelled.[28]

An attentive reader, thinking back to Petrarch's 'Ascent of Mont Ventoux', will have already realized that Petrarch saw Augustine as a model. As Augustine opened a book at random and lit upon a meaningful passage, so too did Petrarch; as Augustine opened the Bible, Petrarch opened Augustine's *Confessions*. Another passage, slightly earlier in that same meaningful chapter of the *Confessions*, saw Augustine wrestling with his sexuality, and he uttered a plea that has become famous: 'Lord,' Augustine implored, 'grant me continence and chastity, but not yet.' Augustine used this episode as a way to show his readers something that in his view was meaningful: he was continually preparing himself for conversion, but his will alone was not enough. It was only when God intervened by turning Augustine's hand to the right biblical passage that he could finally submit and let God's grace enter him. Human will, in other words, was insufficient.

Then, on the other hand, there was Augustine's *City of God*, a book we know was significant to Petrarch: his own copy of this book still exists and was, as it happens, his first recorded book purchase (he tells us in a note on its flyleaf that he bought it in 1325 in Avignon).[29] The *City of God* was a groundbreaking work that, in many ways, set the paradigm for how people thought about history in the Middle Ages: teleologically. This is to say that Augustine proceeded on the assumption that history was, on some level, divinely ordained, that it had a direction and a final ending point, and that one could chart its pattern. Augustine lived when the Roman Empire was ending. He experienced one punctuation mark attesting to the finality of the Empire's decline when the members of a German tribe called the Visigoths invaded Rome in 410. One reason that contemporaries adduced as a cause was the rise of Christianity, a religion whose adherents had abandoned the power of the polytheistic pantheon (in their antagonists' view), focused on the worship of one God and preached personal humility as opposed to public, majestic religious ceremony. Augustine, passionate Christian that he was, countered these ideas with his *City of God*. There, he suggested that God in His infinite wisdom had a plan for human beings and that the plan often included defeats and worldly suffering that did not, on the surface, seem to make sense. Augustine proposed that God's vision encompassed two 'cities': the 'City of Man' – meaning the life of the everyday world, human politics, wars and so on – and the 'City of God' – signifying the regime that will triumph at the end of time, when God's providence so decrees, when the Judgment Day arrives, and when earthly concerns are finally left behind for matters eternal.

So there were two visions behind the *Confessions* and the *City of God*: the necessity of self-scrutiny towards the end of personal conversion, and a vision of history wherein Christianity would eventually triumph and wipe away the world's everyday problems. Both of these visions appealed to Petrarch on a profound level and manifested themselves in his work in different ways.

As to the *Secret*, after Lady Truth is introduced in the work's preface, Petrarch encounters someone whom he recognizes immediately to be Augustine, so much so that

it was not even necessary to ask his name. His religious
aspect, his gentle expression, his serious eyes, his modest gait, his African appearance joined with his Roman
eloquence: these things made it abundantly clear that
it was most glorious Father Augustine.[30]

Henceforth Augustine will function as a guide, a teacher and
a stern taskmaster, whereas Petrarch will be the humble, sometimes wilful, always alert student. This is to say that Augustine
and Petrarch as interlocutors in the dialogue will serve those
functions. Both 'Augustine' ('Augustinus' in the dialogue) and
'Petrarch' ('Franciscus') are, of course, sides of the actual
Petrarch – Petrarch the author – who is writing the dialogue
and using the genre of dialogue in a therapeutic way.

The first book sees Petrarch and Augustine talking about
Petrarch's apparent depression. Augustine urges Petrarch
to embrace virtue and restraint, as the Stoics recommend.
Petrarch agrees that this is what he must do, but is tormented
by the fact that he cannot seem to succeed in that endeavour,
having come to the realization that 'nothing is more difficult to bear than not being able to break the yoke of vice.'[31]
Throughout the three books of the dialogue a most curious
thing happens: Augustine the character diverges from Augustine the historical reality. Augustine the character repeatedly
urges Petrarch (the character) to strengthen his will, as if that
were all that were necessary to overcome his natural tendencies towards vice of different sorts. The actual Augustine
– the real, North African bishop of Hippo who wrote the
Confessions and the *City of God* – had struggled with his vices in
much the same way as had Petrarch. And as we have seen, for

Augustine, the will was not enough for him to be lifted of the burden of vice. It was only after he submitted to God's grace that he was able to free himself and allow God's light to enter him. Petrarch, instead, represents Augustine as a defender of the power of the human will, so that Augustine here and elsewhere in the dialogue has the function of reproving Petrarch. They are not equals – in the literary space of the dialogue, at least – and Augustine serves as the master. By the end of the first book, Augustine offers a diagnosis to Petrarch, to wit: Petrarch has cultivated the ability, in Augustine's view, to recognize what his problems are, even as he has failed to develop the capacity to change.

What, then, were Petrarch's problems? What, in other words, were those tendencies he saw in himself that caused him so much anguish? Just as Augustine had described himself, in the *Confessions*, as being bound by the 'chains' of lust, so too does Petrarch employ the metaphor of chains to refer both to lust and the love of glory. Love and glory: these are Petrarch's weaknesses. To take the latter first, he wants to earn glory from his work, by precisely those enterprises for which he was crowned 'great poet and historian' on the Capitoline Hill in Rome. The second book opens with Augustine warning Petrarch that he is in for a difficult examination, whereupon Petrarch responds that he experiences despair. Augustine retorts that 'despair is the worst of all evils' and that Petrarch must instead gird his soul for the examination to come. Along the way the interlocutors discuss the classics, and specifically what benefit there can be in studying them. Augustine asks how Petrarch's reading of classical literature and philosophy can benefit him if what he reads does not stay with him: 'Go ahead, take pride in your talents. But how has this reading profited you? Out of all the many things you've read, what is it that has lodged itself in your spirit, that has taken root, that has brought forth fruit in a timely manner?'[32] What good is it, Augustine continues, to know facts about the world and 'the secrets of nature, if you remain unknown to yourself?' By the end of the second book it is clear that Augustine (Petrarch's conscience, in other words) sees that the main problem is Petrarch's excessive love of the world and his belief that he might find an easier way to inner peace than the hard road of renunciation.

The side of Petrarch's mind that the interlocutor Augustine represents clearly has an almost obsessive focus on Petrarch as an individual. And it is not that this sort of self-scrutiny was completely unprecedented in Petrarch's era: prayer, confession and spiritual exercise were part and parcel of medieval life. But the level of emotional intensity was unusual, joined as it was to learned, Latinate literary expression. And the tendency to take himself as the most important part of his writing and study is something that pervades all of Petrarch's work. It was all one project, in other words, and in many ways the *Secret* represents a kind of key, something that becomes clear in the third and final book.

After a bit of small talk, Augustine lays out Petrarch's problem for him. It is the point in the dialogue where the 'chains' come up most strongly: 'On your right and left sides, two adamantine chains hold you fast. They prevent you from thinking deeply about either life or death.'[33] Petrarch asks, what are the chains? Augustine answers: 'You know quite well what they are. But, delighted by their beauty, you fail to see them

as chains and instead esteem them to be riches . . . You are
like someone bound on your hands in feet in golden cuffs,
and as you take joy in the gold you fail to see that they are
fetters.'[34] Petrarch responds: 'What then are these two chains
to which you point?' Augustine: 'Love and glory.'

First, then, there was love and specifically, Petrarch's love
for Laura, which – Augustine charges – has so obsessed Petrarch that it has caused him to turn his heart and soul towards
a creature rather than the Creator. Petrarch counters that in
his love for Laura, there was 'never anything wicked, nothing
carnal, nothing, finally, beyond how great his love was that is
worthy of blame'.[35] Augustine however is not persuaded,
arguing that Petrarch's love for Laura diminished him: 'What
a great man you might have become, had she not held you
back with the allure of her beauty' (illus. 15).[36] Petrarch continues to fight back, replying that he always loved Laura's soul
most of all. But Augustine will have none of it. And then, in
a move that seems to foreshadow Charles Dickens's 'ghost of
Christmas past', Augustine takes Petrarch back to his childhood, and he asks him the most difficult question of all: 'Do
you remember how great was your fear of God in that time
of life, how frequently you thought of death, how dear religion was to you, and how great was your love for integrity?'[37]
Petrarch is caught up short, and his reply is affecting: 'I
remember indeed. And it pains me that, as the years have
gone by, these virtues have waned.'[38] A few lines later Petrarch
admits the truth: that after he saw and fell in love with Laura,
'I was diverted and placed on a path that was indirect and
unclean, and though I have often looked back through my
tears, I have been unable to stick to the straight way. And it

is true: when I left it, then – especially then – that was when my moral confusion began.'[39]

Remember that both 'Petrarch' and 'Augustine' are one person, Petrarch himself, whose suffering and intense self-scrutiny are evident. What is it that Petrarch laments here? On the surface, it is the way in which the sight of a beautiful woman, when young, awakened in him emotions and passions that did not sit well with the idealized, meditative Christian life he sees as best. But in a deeper and more lasting fashion, it has to do with the passage of time, the way in which ageing blunts youthful ideals, and those moments in life when we encounter crossroads. Those crossroads always imply decisions and, the older one gets, the more one realizes that making this or that decision precludes other possibilities. As Book 3 progresses, in fact, one realizes that this sense of a momentous decision in Petrarch's life is before him. Yet, Petrarch being Petrarch, even as one part of his decision will become clear, other matters will remain unresolved, as we shall see.

First and foremost, the emotional level rises. Augustine does not cease reminding Petrarch of how much inner turmoil and suffering his love for Laura has caused him, to what vanities it has propelled him, and how much he has lost control of himself. It is because of his love for Laura, Augustine accuses, that Petrarch has experienced 'pallor, meagerness, and the very flowering of youth fading away, eyes that are always wet and besieged by concern, a mind that is jumbled and sleep robbed of rest', and so on. 'Do these seem to you to be signs of good health?' Petrarch, through his love for Laura, came to lose control of himself: 'A change in her expression changed

your spirit, and you became happy or sad simply on account
of her fickleness. In the final analysis, you depended entirely
on her will.'[40] Augustine presses on, and in so doing gives us
yet another tantalizing glimpse into Petrarch and the place
that his possessions held in his life: 'What could be crazier
than this: not satisfied with the presence of her face – that
very face that brought all of this on – you had another version
of her face made by an illustrious artist, so that, carrying it
around everywhere with you, you might always have material
for never-ending tears.'[41] This is true: although it is lost today,
Petrarch commissioned Simone Martini, the very same artist
who had done the frontispiece in the 'Ambrosian Virgil', to
do a portrait of Laura, small and on paper, that Petrarch could
carry around in his travels.[42] He mentions the portrait in two
of his poems in the *Canzoniere*, with one allusion being especially noteworthy: 'To be sure my Simone was in paradise,
whence this noble lady comes; he saw her there and portrayed
her on paper, to attest down here to her lovely face.'[43] As in
the case of the 'Ambrosian Virgil', Petrarch memorialized
Laura and made her portable.

   In the rhythms of the *Secret*, Laura serves as more than just
a figure of lament: she becomes a literary device, allowing
Petrarch to make the transition to his next topic: glory, and
the manner in which his search for glory was stimulated –
so he says – by his vision of Laura and by her qualities as a
muse. Yet again, Petrarch (the author) has the strongest cri-
tiques come out of the mouth of Augustine (the interlocutor).
Petrarch, 'Augustine' accuses, became so enamoured of Laura's
name that he then subsequently became obsessed with anything that sounded like it and hence with the idea of the

15 Illumination by Francesco di Antonio del Chierico in a 1476 parchment copy of Petrarch's *Canzoniere* that depicts Petrarch avoiding drowning from shipwreck by clinging to an olive branch.

'imperial or the poetic laurel'. And so, 'since it was out of the question to hope for the imperial laurel, you then lusted after the poetic laurel – something for which the level of your researches held out hope – no less arrogantly than you had fallen for the Lady herself'.[44]

Out of the question. The expression used in Latin for that formulation is *non fas erat*, which at the most literal level means 'it was not lawful.' Is Petrarch subtly signalling regret for his ill-advised support of Cola, regret expressed only to himself? Is he somehow doubting the seeming confidence with which he had in 1341 staged his own elaborate laureation, in which at the symbolic level he linked poetry and politics? It would be impossible to say definitively, of course, but the sense of self-doubt that runs through the *Secret* grows ever more in its intensity as the work progresses. It reaches a kind of apogee, as well. Having made the transition from love to glory, having in fact suggested that they were, for him, linked – that Laura's beauty had spurred him on and impelled his search – he moves to a discussion focused on glory and, ultimately, on the possibility of departure.

The first step is Petrarch's qualified admission that his love for Laura has not been good for him. He admits that he has been, in effect, addicted to her. Still, he speaks forcefully to Augustine: 'Know this: I can love in no other way. My spirit has become accustomed to wonder at her, just as my eyes have grown used to regarding her and deeming anything else unpleasant and full of shadow.'[45] The question becomes, what to do? At first, the answer seems to be travel, flight from the habitual place, Avignon, that has been the source of so much inner turmoil. Petrarch mentions that he has tried to flee, but that these attempts have had no appreciable effect on his level of agitation. He asks Augustine what good travel will do if his soul is not cured. Augustine responds in a telling fashion, regarding the soul: 'I did not say that the soul must be cured, or healed, but rather that it must be prepared.'[46] This notion of 'preparing' the soul is crucial, both for the interlocutor, Augustine, and for Petrarch, the author and person. It forms part of a tradition in the history of philosophy that has not always been recognized adequately, given its importance: the tradition of spiritual exercises and, more specifically in this case, the way in which the culture of reading and writing often intersected with that tradition.

The idea, which runs throughout the history of philosophy broadly conceived, finds expression in the work of Plato, in the history of Christianity (most especially in Augustine's *Confessions* and the Jesuit 'Spiritual Exercises'), and, in truth, in a number of non-Western traditions.[47] It is this: you can improve yourself by focusing on your own character, finding its flaws and consciously trying to correct them. As to reading and writing, for Petrarch, the very act of writing his struggles down, of posing arguments pro and contra, represented a powerful way to accomplish this end of self-improvement.[48] Take what the character Augustine says in the *Secret*: 'This, then, is what I advise, what I urge, what I command: the spirit must be taught to put aside all those things that press upon it and, then, without hope of return, depart. It is only then that you will understand how powerful absence can be when it comes to spiritual healing.'[49] In effect, Augustine is telling Petrarch – and Petrarch is of course telling himself – something seemingly simple but profoundly important: wherever you go,

there you are. No travel will help you unless you can put behind you those things that have held you back.

As it happens what is holding Petrarch back is not only
Laura but the way that outward signs can trigger unhealthy
responses in one who is not prepared to resist them. Augustine
admonishes Petrarch: 'Seeing the purple' – traditionally the
colour worn by powerful politicians – 'on someone else's back
renews ambition; the sight of a little pile of coins revitalizes
greed; the glimpse of a body's beauty can inflame lust; and the
smallest batting of the eyes awakens a love that had been
asleep.'[50] It is about the senses, about perception, about how
what one experiences in day-to-day life can lead to thinking
and behaviour that will only be a cause for regret. Augustine's
advice for Petrarch (provided Petrarch can keep the care of his
soul in mind) is that he must leave and find new surroundings.
Petrarch agrees, but says he is 'uncertain as to where I might
best go'. Augustine replies that he is well aware that Italy has
always been Petrarch's dream, that he has praised it in one of
his poems as a place beautiful like no other.[51] Augustine says
Italy is a place where Petrarch can enjoy the habits of its
people and beauty of its geography. So: 'Just go and be happy,
wherever your spirit takes you. Go untroubled, and hurry
and don't look back! Forget the past, look towards what is to
come. You have been exiled from your homeland – and from
yourself – for far too long. It is time to return.'[52] The self-
identification as an exile and the identification of self with
Italy ('from your homeland and yourself') have become an
integral part of who Petrarch is by this point in his life.

As the dialogue progresses it becomes clear that a shift had
taken place: Petrarch is convinced that his move to Italy is

imminent. But Augustine still seems to believe that Petrarch needs more spiritual training. This time it has to do with the relative impermanence of human life and the way that taking note of the manner in which we age can lead to more mature reflection on our place in the universe. 'So let me ask you this,' Augustine queries: 'Haven't you noticed that your face changes day by day and that ever more grey hair emerges as time goes by?'[53] Surprised, Petrarch responds that it is obvious that people age, even if it seems to him that people are ageing ever faster. Once more in the position of stern master, Augustine tells Petrarch not to worry about others but to focus on himself. Augustine asks Petrarch what he thinks about ageing and what he has to say. Petrarch responds with a host of examples from ancient literature that point to or have to do with ageing. Augustine grows impatient: 'I tell you to think about ageing, and instead you bring forth a crowd of famous old men. What can this mean?'[54] Petrarch's natural tendency – this holds true both for the character in the dialogue and the author himself – is to look reflexively towards antiquity whenever a question arises.

In this case Augustine's question had to do with ageing, and Petrarch's reflex was to look towards examples of ancients who had aged well and who thus could serve as models for how to achieve glory. They became part of literary and cultural memory and were worthy of commemoration long after their deaths. Augustine will have none of it, and he wastes no time in bringing Petrarch back to earth. His first move is to suggest that, even still, Petrarch in some respects remains, if not a child, addicted to childlike pursuits. He needs to understand that 'days fly away, the body decays, but the spirit remains unchanged.'[55] And more: 'Childhood flies, but childishness remains. And you – believe me – you are by no means so young as you might think. Most men do not reach the age at which you find yourself.'[56] A stern Augustine goes on to tell Petrarch he should be ashamed to be known as an old man who is still lovestruck. 'So put away boyish ineptitude.'

Augustine then gives Petrarch, the 'Renaissance man', a lecture that might have fitted in any number of medieval spiritual exercises, so potent that it is worthy of quoting extensively. 'Think then first of all,' Augustine admonishes,

> about the nobility of the soul, which is so great that, were I to want to discourse upon it, I would need to retrace my entire book. Think about the fragility and the foulness of the human body, which are one and the same, and about which there would be material no less copious to treat. Think about the brevity of life, a theme on which there are books by great men. Think about the passage of time, to which no one can do justice in words. Think about the utter certainty of death and the uncertain hour of death, something that, at any time, in any place, impends. Think about this one thing about which all men are mistaken: they think that they can put off what cannot be put off . . .[57]

It is all about death, and Augustine urges Petrarch to remember that every day must be thought of as if it were or could be one's last. On one hand, this tendency can be linked to how close Petrarch was to the Black Death. On the other, it is important to recognize that Petrarch – the author, not the character – is engaging here in a classic spiritual exercise, in which one trains one's own mind by stretching it, as it were, by remembering what one knows to be most important, and by writing.

This linking of personal spiritual growth to writing is a tendency that reaches back to Marcus Aurelius, the Roman emperor who wrote in Greek and plumbed the depths of his inner thoughts for no one's edification but his own.[58] His *Meditations* survived the tests of time, but, much like Petrarch's *Secret*, were not necessarily written for public consumption. The fact that Petrarch works through his concerns and moves his own spiritual exercise forwards is a little paradoxical, given the dialogue's most powerfully interesting section: its critique of writing as a means to gain glory. For this is precisely that to which Augustine next points. He singles out Petrarch's writing, focusing on the works which, one suspects, Petrarch believed might gain him lasting glory: his *On Illustrious Men* and his *Africa*. By the time Petrarch was writing his *Secret*, he had already put a fair amount of work into both projects, so it is worth pausing a while to understand them.

On Illustrious Men was a collection of biographies of ancient figures thought to be exemplary, in the sense that studying their lives could teach modern readers virtue (illus. 16). Petrarch took great care with this work and, in compiling it, exercised his scholarly abilities – and the craft of the historian – to maximum effect. Indeed, Petrarch, in the preface to that work, wrote both about the goals at hand and about reconciling sources that might be in conflict. In so doing, he also helped create a new idea of what it was that historians should endeavour to do:

I have decided . . . to collect or rather almost to compress into one place the praise of the illustrious men who flourished with outstanding glory and whose memory – which I found spread far and wide and scattered in sundry volumes – has been handed to us through the skill of many learned men.[59]

16 Portrait of Petrarch by Altichiero da Verona in a 1379 copy of Petrarch's *De viris illustribus.*

On the one hand, this notion (that one should gather together accounts of the deeds of great men from disparate sources) was familiar, present both in ancient sources and in the work of Petrarch's contemporaries. On the other, Petrarch spends enough time on the topic that it becomes clear that his 'method' was important to him. For example, he writes:

> For although the things I am going to write about are found in other authors, they are not, however, found collected there in the same way. For what is lacking in one author I have supplied from another . . . I have joined together many things which were found dispersed in many histories, by one author or by several, and I have made them a whole . . . I am neither the peacemaker among conflicting historians nor the collector of every minute fact; but rather, I am the copier of those whose verisimilitude or greater authority demands that they be given greater credence.[60]

The reader gathers a number of impressions.

First, comparison forms a key part of this method, meaning that the goal is not to find one source for an ancient event and use only that source as a basis. Rather, competing accounts must be weighed one against the other, so that plausibility, chronology and reliability can all be taken into account. Petrarch is interested only in ancient information (as we have seen, he believed that contemporary princes 'offer material suitable not so much for history but rather for satire'). Needless to say, there is no question of his being a 'modern' historian: he is not using archival sources, and he is relatively uninterested in other sorts of evidence that historians now use to reconstruct the ancient world, like inscriptions, coins or archaeological remains. Still, Petrarch's thinking here, and the method that it reflects, can be seen as a seed that, once planted, could grow and branch out. Italian Renaissance thinkers after him would go on to write a lot of history, much of which would surpass Petrarch's attempts in terms of expertise. But this basic idea – that no single authority was unable to be challenged and that one needed to be broadly comparative, employing as many sources as needed – became one of the hallmarks of scholarly life in the period. And of course (to return to Petrarch and his own psychology) *On Illustrious Men* was a work that he hoped would win him glory.

The same went for his *Africa*, and the same basic inspiration – to focus attention on the triumphs and exemplary leaders of ancient Rome – was in play. Also in play was the use of history, and in this case especially Livy's history of ancient Rome. In fact, precisely some of the parts of Livy's text that Petrarch had worked so hard to restore (specifically, Livy's third 'decade') emerged as important in the composition of the *Africa*. For the story told there was that of the second Punic War, a key part of ancient Rome's expansion when it was a growing republic in the later third century BCE, when it fought against the north African city of Carthage (in today's Tunisia). It was a war that featured magnificent episodes and great characters, not least among them the African general Hannibal, who after landing with his forces in Spain made his way through France and then, memorably, crossed the Alps with his army, some of whom were borne on elephants. Opposing him was another celebrated general, the Roman Scipio, who had suffered early defeats against the Carthaginians and then, against the advice of some of Rome's leading figures, took forces with him into Carthage, where he defeated Hannibal at the battle of Zama in 202 BCE. It was the turning point in Rome's long conflict with Carthage. At its end, the terms imposed on the losing Carthaginians were severe enough that they were henceforth no longer a threat to Rome's ambitions. When Scipio returned to Rome, he was awarded the honour of a 'triumph' – a procession and public ceremony where, habitually, a winning general was feted, as he wore a laurel crown and purple vestments. Scipio was given the extra name of *Africanus* – 'the African' – in honour of his victories. Thereafter he settled back into an initially apolitical life and then, when partisan Roman politics became too difficult to bear, he retired to a country estate in southern Italy.

Many themes in the story of Scipio's life resonated with Petrarch: the defence of peninsular Italy from outsiders and the expansion of Roman power; the virtuous military conduct in battle; and perhaps even the fact that Scipio spent at least a part of his life unappreciated by his home city – an 'outsider' like Petrarch. The *Africa* was to include all those themes and more. And there were two distinguishing features about the *Africa*: it was to be in Latin, and it was consciously an epic poem, with Virgil's *Aeneid* and its graceful Latin hexameters as a model. As to the fact that it was in Latin, in one respect this is unsurprising: Petrarch elsewhere wrote that he saw Latin as the 'root of all of our arts', and it was clearly the language he saw as lasting, one that could serve as an 'official' language to deal with matters needing serious commemoration.[61] Moreover, an earlier northern Italian literary figure,

Albertino Mussato of Padua (1261–1329), had written a Latin epic poem in a self-consciously classicizing (rather than medieval) Latin style, though that poem, the *Ecerinis*, had to do with the exploits of a recent figure, the tyrant and strongman Ezzelino da Romano (1194–1259).[62]

But in this case, there was also the fact that Dante's *Comedy* had already become an acknowledged classic by the time Petrarch first started work on the *Africa*. Dante's *Comedy* was not a historical epic, of course. But it was there, always in the back of Petrarch's mind, so much so that in letters with his friend Boccaccio, Petrarch does not mention Dante's name even when Dante is under discussion. There will be more to say about this relationship, but for now it is enough to know that Dante was like a ghost in the back of Petrarch's mind, one with which he was always in competition. And then there was the matter of Virgil, whose *Aeneid* was the founding epic poem of Latin literature, one that told the story of Rome's beginnings in language that was absorbing and beautiful. So there were imposing models behind Petrarch's work. There were differences when compared to the Virgilian model: Virgil's *Aeneid* had twelve books, whereas the *Africa* had only nine. And Virgil told a tale that integrated myth, history and subtle political commentary in a manner so compelling that the *Aeneid* became, and has remained, a classic of world literature.

Petrarch's *Africa* never had that kind of success. In fact, he never quite finished it, shadowed as he was by the twin mountains of Virgil and Dante, one ancient, one modern, both having written works that all acknowledged were worthy of eternal esteem. Today, the *Africa* is generally considered a failure as a work of epic poetry. But a look beneath the surface shows us that it holds great importance in understanding Petrarch's goals and outlook. In some respects, the demands of the kind of epic Petrarch wanted to write did not quite fit with the society in which he found himself. In Virgil's *Aeneid*, for example, the gods regularly intervened in human affairs. Aeneas himself was half divine (Venus was his mother). And it was Juno's deep-seated hatred of Troy, Aeneas's home, that served as an engine for many of the *Aeneid*'s plot points. For Petrarch, in a Christian context where there was one God alone, it was difficult to have that kind of action take place; he did include a 'council of the gods' that he tried to Christianize, whose members deliberated over earthly matters. But it was a difficult fit and does not quite work, serving more as something that distracts a reader. In many respects Petrarch saw his *Africa* as a counterpart to his *On Illustrious Men*: both would teach virtue to readers by example, and both would uncover overlooked but important parts of ancient Roman history. Even in this latter respect, however, critics have accused Petrarch of, essentially, versifying Livy's third 'Decade', telling in not so melodious poetry what Livy had expressed in enduring Latin prose.

Whatever its flaws, the *Africa* opens a window onto Petrarch's view of poetry and his hoped-for place in its history. As to his view of poetry and what it should do, Petrarch makes his thoughts known through the mouth of a poet who is today little known, Ennius (239–169 BCE), who had lived during the war which the *Africa* describes. Towards the end of the *Africa*, Ennius says:

Poets do not possess the kind of warrant that allows them openly to please the many. One must first lay down the most solid foundations of truth. Leaning on these foundations, he can hide himself under a cloud both beautiful and diverse, preparing for a reader a labor that is lengthy and in need of quiet. For the reader, the harder it is to discover the real meaning, the sweeter it is to find it.[63]

The poet must be able to see and survey everything that occurs in life – the cultivation of virtue, the study of the natural world – and he must then conceal them underneath 'a cloak that will cover them' or 'under a light veil'.[64]

The language is arresting. On the one hand, the idea that there was a core of truth in poetry that was hidden and that needed to be brought forward by careful, quiet interpretation was an old one. It formed a key part of the way learned readers in antiquity encountered poetry. With the rise of Christianity, this interpretive tendency became even more important, as medieval thinkers found multiple levels of meaning in scripture, one that was literal and on the surface, and a series of others whose meaning needed to be dug out.[65] On the other hand, it was also a commonplace that poets had a certain licence with the truth. It is not that Petrarch is denying that characterization here. But he is overtly suggesting that a firm foundation of truth must underlie poetry. Petrarch is thinking of his own poetry in the *Africa*: it must contain truth, it should possess alluring beauty across many interpretive layers and it must, accordingly, be something whose most important, deepest meanings are reserved for a select few readers, who have the time, intelligence and inclination to understand that good poetry takes work on the part of both the writer and the reader.

It is striking that Petrarch uses the poet Ennius as a mouth-piece. True, Ennius was a contemporary of Scipio Africanus, the *Africa*'s great hero. In that respect there is a chronological legitimacy to his presence. But neither Petrarch nor we possess anything but tiny fragments of what Ennius had written. Then and now, what Ennius had was a reputation, as one who had learned from ancient Greek models. He thus served as one of the first major Latin writers to find the 'sweet spot' between imitating the acknowledged cultural primacy of the Greeks and then culturally translating Greek ideas for Roman audiences in an original way. Ennius' presence also tells us much about Petrarch's vision of himself in the genealogy of poetry.

First, and along these lines, absences are as important as presences, and the major absence here is the poet Virgil, something that becomes clear soon after Ennius discourses on the value of poetry. Ennius looks back at the history of poetry, relating something that came to him in a dream. He says that he had been brought back to 'the earliest shades, indeed the first men', whom fame had left forgotten.[66] As he did so he arrived at one in particular, Homer, who seemed from his qualities to have come from heaven itself, so much so, Ennius continues, 'that I am stunned that a mortal man could reach such heights'.[67] Homer becomes Ennius' guide in the dream vision, and as Ennius's eyes light upon an arresting sight, he asks Homer for an explanation of what they see before them. Ennius narrates:

Here I said – for I saw a young man sitting in an enclosed valley – 'O my most respected leader, whosoever is this, sitting as he thinks deeply among the delicate laurels, wreathing his head with blooming branch? If I am not mistaken, there is something outstanding and high-minded deep within his heart, upon which he is meditating.'[68]

It is not too difficult to guess where this is going. Homer responds to Ennius: 'You are not mistaken at all. You see a late descendant of our race' – meaning the 'race' or 'class' of poets – 'whom the region of Italy will bring forth in the final era of mankind. Etruscan Florence, arising from the roots planted by Romulus, will with its wide walls bring him forth. And though it is nothing now, that city will in future become famous.'[69]

Before he reveals to Ennius who this poet is, Homer has more to tell:

In the final era, that man will restore the ancient sisters [the Muses] to Helicon, though he will experience different disturbances in his life. His name will be Franciscus, and he will make everything you see around you famous, gathering everything as he will into one work: the battles in Spain, the Lybian labours, and everything that has to do with the actions of your Scipio. The title of his poem will be AFRICA.[70]

As to absences, then, two major names are missing: Virgil and of course Dante. The Muses, presumably, were still active in

Virgil's day. And yet Petrarch simply jumps from Homer and Ennius all the way to his own era. Petrarch loved Virgil, of course, as he says numerous times elsewhere in his work. But in his own *Africa*, it seems that even to mention the great Roman poet might have come as a threat. Then, by claiming for himself the privilege of restoring the Muses to their rightful place, Petrarch implies that Dante's great work could not have done the rightful job of restoration. More positively we can say that Petrarch is suggesting that he hopes to do something new.

In all of the above, a few elements come to the fore. First there is the reference to Mount Helicon, which we can pair with Petrarch's oration that he composed for his laureation ceremony on Rome's Capitoline Hill, and more specifically with the quotation from Virgil with which Petrarch opened that work: *sed me Parnasi deserta per ardua dulcis / raptat amor*: 'It is love that compels me upward, over the lonely slopes of Parnassus.'[71] Both Parnassus and Helicon were considered homes of the Muses, sacred spaces that served symbolically as the protection for poetry and the arts. Petrarch's foregrounding of Virgil's quotation in his oration and his mention of Helicon here in the *Africa* both show that he believed there was a lacuna in modern culture having to do with serious cultivation of poetry and that he was the person to fill that lacuna.

Second, and again as to absences, Ennius' mention of Florence is noteworthy. It signals that Petrarch, though absent from that city almost his whole life, still felt compelled to claim it as his place of origin. The presence of Florence, like so much else in Petrarch's work, points us to his own, lifelong search for who he really was and where his identity was to be located, both geographically and within a landscape of other famous literary figures. Finally, we observe, in Homer and Ennius' conversation about Petrarch sitting in a 'closed valley' (*clausa . . . valle*, in Latin, meaning 'Vaucluse'), that 'there is something outstanding and high-minded, deep within his heart'. In the course of the *Africa* that sentiment serves to predict that Petrarch will author poetry that will tell Scipio Africanus' story. But it has a larger significance as well: Petrarch believed his work was destined for greatness, if not in this life, then in years to come.

Soon thereafter, Ennius and Homer notice something else about the young poet, imbued with so much potential. Homer tells Ennius: *Quin etiam ingenii fiducia quanta, quantus aget laudum stimulus*, or 'How much faith he' – Petrarch, in other words – 'puts in his own genius, how much praise goads him on!' Homer then predicts that Petrarch will be honoured with a triumph on the Capitoline Hill, so inspired will he be by 'love and reverence for the laurel'. Petrarch's love of 'Laura' and the 'laurel', the way he places himself in view of two ancient poets and the manner in which the desire to revive ancient ceremony in the modern age becomes a priority: all emerge from his allusive hexameters.

Perhaps most important, however, is Petrarch's self-consciousness of his own desire for glory. For that is – to close this lengthy parenthesis on the *Africa* – the real struggle with which he engages in his *Secret*. To return to that work, to its third and final book, and to the character Augustine's chastisement of the character Petrarch: it is precisely with a discussion of glory that the *Secret* concludes. Augustine asks Petrarch if he knows what glory is. Petrarch, humbly, asks Augustine to explain. Augustine paraphrases Cicero to the effect that glory is 'fame' or 'renown' (*fama*, in Latin), 'among one's fellow citizens, homeland, and every race of men'.[72] The question then becomes, what is fame? Again, Petrarch defers to Augustine, and this time, Augustine is calculatedly stern in his discourse. 'Know therefore', Augustine says, 'that fame is nothing other than speech about someone that is common and sprinkled about on the mouths of the many.'[73] So far, so good. It all sounds very neutral. But Augustine presses on, suggesting that this sort of speech is nothing more than 'a flighty puff of air'.[74]

Petrarch replies that he understands this seemingly ephemeral nature of speech but that he is still stimulated to achieve glory: he is here on earth now, after all, and it seems like a natural thing. Even if 'fame' is something that in a contemporary sense is evanescent, it is still something worthy. Augustine divines Petrarch's real purpose: 'You haven't been satisfied with your every-day work . . . projecting your thoughts far into the future as you do, you have desired fame among those who are yet to come.'[75] Augustine then zeroes in on the two works upon which Petrarch has pinned his hopes.

First, there is *On Illustrious Men*, 'a work that is gigantic and that takes as much time and work as one can imagine'. Augustine goes on: 'And even though that work had not yet been brought to a conclusion, you were driven by such spurs of glory that you boarded a kind of poetic boat for Africa.'[76] The language Augustine uses here, in the *Secret*, to describe Petrarch's desire for glory is similar to that which 'Homer' had used in the *Africa* when the ancient Greek bard saw the young poet who would, millennia hence, form part of a succession of divine poetic expositors of matters of moment. In both cases the key word is the Latin *stimulus*, which can signify what it looks like in English but which can also mean 'goad' or 'spur', both meanings that are associated with the language of horsemanship. This is what glory and fame are like, for Petrarch: he is the horse, and glory and fame are what spur him on. In any case the similar language in both the *Africa* and the *Secret* shows us where Petrarch was at this middle point of his life: engaged in the pursuit of glory based on Latin letters and yet conflicted by that very commitment.

As the *Secret* winds to its conclusion, death is on the interlocutors' minds. So many factors impede even a famous name remaining so for long. Death is the primary impediment, as Augustine tells Petrarch: 'First of all there is the death of all of those men with whom one has transacted one's life. And then there is forgetfulness, a natural evil accompanying old age.'[77] Beyond all this there is also the tendency of people to praise younger men, who are always attempting to show up those who are older; there is the inconstancy of the judgement of the many; and then there is the way in which even graves and sepulchres fall, something that Petrarch himself, in his *Africa*, called a 'second death' (as Augustine is quick to remind him). And although books might seem to have a longer life, they too are, in the final analysis, subject to all the forms of destruction and oblivion present elsewhere. Books, in other words – Petrarch's own books – will eventually be forgotten and unavailable. In some small respect this latter sentiment reflects a real concern in the pre-modern world, whose members simply could not imagine the relative abundance of books amid which we live today. More broadly, this injunction against putting one's faith in books as portals to personal fame represents the central core of Petrarch's struggle with his literary work and with his difficulty in bringing projects to completion.

Indeed, this problem becomes clear, as Petrarch – having heard all of Augustine's talk of death and dying and abandoning the things of this world – asks plaintive questions:

> What then should I do? Should I just abandon my projects, after having interrupted them? Or should I instead, speed them up and, with God's blessing, finish them so that, relieved of these concerns I might proceed with greater exposition to more important matters?[78]

Augustine's answer, finally, is twofold and simple: 'Cast off the weighty shackles of your historical work. The deeds of the Romans and their consequent fame have been amply illustrated by the talents of others.' Second and more probingly, Augustine continues: 'Put Africa aside, and leave it to those who possess it. You'll gain glory neither for Scipio nor for yourself: he cannot be praised any more highly, and you'll just struggle along after him on a side street.'[79] *Dimitte Africam*: 'Put Africa aside.' This was the epic Petrarch had been inspired to write as he dreamed of his laurel crown, on which he continued to work after receiving it, and with which he was still, at the time of his *Secret*, preoccupied. The rest of the dialogue has some more back and forth, but the two injunctions regarding *On Illustrious Men* and the *Africa* represent the core of the interlocutor Augustine's message to the interlocutor Petrarch. And, of course, they emblematize Petrarch's own struggle.

The dialogue ends with Petrarch still in a state of ambivalence. Admitting that Augustine's advice – to leave his work behind and work instead on his own soul – is the right thing to do, Petrarch says that, though he would like to do so, 'I am unable to refrain my desire.'[80] Augustine responds: 'We are falling back into our old debate – you designate the will as powerless,' meaning that Petrarch in Augustine's estimation is abdicating control over his will and that, if he really wanted to do so, he could indeed pursue the path Augustine has outlined for him.[81] Again, we have a representation of Augustine that is only that, a representation, as Augustine himself was acutely conscious of the weakness of the human will. But Petrarch is not trying to offer a systematic account of Augustine's thoughts on the human will. Instead Petrarch is projecting one side of his personality and one part of his interior conflicts onto the page. The two sides would always be there for him, always a part of who he was: interior versus exterior, contemplative versus active, a man in retreat versus a man on the move.

And on the move he was. After drafting his *Secret*, surviving the plague, outliving the real biographical Laura (even if her image remained ever with him) and, finally, surveying the remains of his life in France, he made the momentous decision to move to Italy, something he did definitively in 1353. Offered patronage by the archbishop of Milan, Giovanni Visconti (1290–1354), Petrarch decamped for Milan. A metrical letter he composed gives us a sense of his excitement:

O, our Italy! Greetings, my dear Italy, greetings, land that is most holy in the eyes of God, land that is protected by its possessions, a land to be feared by the proud, a land nobler, more fertile and more beautiful than any other, girded by a twin sea [the Adriatic and the Mediterranean] a land famous for its renowned mountains, a land to be honoured for its glory in arms, for its sacred laws, a land that is the home of the Muses and rich in treasures and heroes, a land whose art and nature kept for themselves the highest applause and at the same time made Italy the teacher of the whole world. Now, desirous as I have been for a long time to do so, I return to you, to be an inhabitant forever . . .[82]

Clearly, Petrarch was happy about the move. In these years, too, Petrarch developed one of the most significant relationships of his life.

FIVE

A Life in Letters: Petrarch and Boccaccio

LREADY THERE IS NO LAND, no sky that remain mine, nor am I a resident anywhere. And so I am everywhere a wanderer."[1] Petrarch wrote these words in a metrical Latin letter to a friend, and they can stand as a statement representing his constant need to seek out new places, new people and new cultural environments. A reader has probably inferred enough already to know that he was fully satisfied in none of these places. Petrarch had one of those natures that, though it rendered him capable of experiencing great joy, also often led to intense dissatisfaction. Indeed, in another section of the *Secret*, 'Augustine' and 'Franciscus' engaged in a lengthy discussion of Petrarch's *aegritudo* or *acedia*, both words that can mean 'listlessness' but which we can recognize today as depression. His predilection to travel in the hopes of dispelling that *aegritudo* never left him, not even after 1353, the year that signalled his permanent move to Italy.

There was one thing, however, that remained a steady source of psychological nourishment throughout Petrarch's travels: his friendship with Giovanni Boccaccio. Boccaccio, traditionally considered a follower of Petrarch, became a lot more than that: an admirer turned confidant, one of Petrarch's best friends and a catalyst for Petrarch's work. Petrarch had met Boccaccio for the first time in Florence when travelling to Rome for a great papal celebration (called a jubilee and held at regular intervals) in 1350. A year after that first meeting Petrarch found himself in Padua, near Venice, where Boccaccio, at his own expense, visited Petrarch in the hope that he might be lured to Florence with the offer of a professorship at the University of Florence. Boccaccio had arranged this offer with university officials, and on it he had hung great hopes. But it was not to be, as Petrarch was not ready for that kind of commitment, even though it would have brought him officially within the orbit of the city, Florence, that he considered so important in his own genealogy. Despite Boccaccio's failed attempt to lure Petrarch to Florence, however, their relationship grew ever stronger emotionally, through Petrarch's most important means of self-expression: letters. There are eighteen letters between the two men, which chart their continuing evolution together, as they discuss literature and (sometimes in a hidden fashion, sometimes more openly) the presence of Dante.

The correspondence of Petrarch and Boccaccio would be worth a book in itself. Boccaccio, about ten years younger than Petrarch, idolized the older scholar. And Petrarch, as senior partners in these sorts of relationships often do, worked out his own anxieties and concerns in the presence of an adoring admirer, one towards whom he displayed the persona of friend, father, and brother. A look at three of these letters proves revealing, both to see how Petrarch situated himself when he was in his full maturity, and to chart how the beginnings of an Italian literary canon were being formed.

The first letter has to do with an unnamed poet towards whom Petrarch is supposed by some to feel envy. Boccaccio had earlier written Petrarch a letter that had, as Petrarch deemed it, two matters within it that demanded a response. The tenor of Petrarch's language is, if not heated, at least emotionally charged:

> First of all, you ask pardon, and that in an eager fashion, for seeming to have praised a fellow countryman – certainly someone who is agreeable to the multitude in respect of his style and who is, to be sure, an out-standing poet in reality – overmuch. And indeed you justify yourself in such a way that you make it seem that praise for him or for anyone at all takes away from praise for me. You go on to claim that, if I look care-fully at whatever you say about him, it will redound to my glory. You add expressly that the reason for your courtesy towards him has to do with the fact that he was the first guide of your studies when you were a very young man, the first light, as it were.[2]

We can note, first of all, that the unnamed author around whom all of this fraught conversation swirled was, of course, Dante. Petrarch never names Dante, but his presence in Pet-rarch's psychology is undeniable. Petrarch's language in the letter is noteworthy. The single Latin word translated here as 'agreeable to the multitude' is *popularis*, a word that has a number of shades of meaning. Most neutrally, it means 'of the people'. In the sense Petrarch is using it here, it also signifies the language 'of the people' – the vernacular, in other words, a language to which Petrarch had a complicated relation, as we will see revealed in other letters. The fact that Petrarch juxtaposes the word *popularis* with a positive affirmation of Dante as a poet (Dante, 'who is, to be sure, an outstanding poet in reality') is also revealing: it suggests that Petrarch's feelings about things that were *popularis*, language included, were in fact not neutral and that anything that might appeal to the multitude came, as such, under suspicion of being trivial and insufficiently complex to be meaningful.

Petrarch also discloses that he was quite conscious of his own reputation:

> Now those who hate me claim that I hate or despise him, so that they might induce the crowd – among whom he is quite well liked – to hate me. This is a novel kind of wickedness and a wondrous craft of causing pain. So let the truth itself serve as my response.[3]

Petrarch was a known figure by this point, and as in the case of all such people, there would have been those who wanted to take him down a few notches. Still, one wonders how much chatter there really was, and how much these words represent emotional fragility on Petrarch's part. First, Petrarch asks how there can be any cause for hatred towards a man 'who appeared only once to me, and at my earliest boyhood at that'.[4] As to the 'truth itself', Petrarch tells Boccaccio that Ser Petracco, Petrarch's father, and Dante lived in Florence at the same time and shared the fate of exile for political reasons. And so, 'as you see, there is nothing to cause hatred and, instead, much to cause love', since they came ultimately from the same homeland.[5] Those unnamed notional slanderers, in other words, who try to suggest without foundation that Petrarch had anything against Dante should take into account that there were deep ties already between the two families whence Dante and Petrarch hailed.

His (perhaps hypothetical?) accusers also say that, though Petrarch had always had a passion for collecting books, 'I never had his book' – the *Divine Comedy* – 'and though I was most eager in collecting all the others, indeed seeking some that were almost hopeless to find, with respect to that one, which was indeed new and easy to obtain, I was, in a way that was different for me and not my usual habit, rather indifferent.'[6] Petrarch's book-hunting habits were so well known that anyone would wonder why he never had a copy of 'his book' (*librum illius* – 'the book of that one', most literally, straining in both Latin and English to avoid any mention of the title or author). And this, Petrarch confesses, was indeed true: desiring to become a great vernacular writer, he avoided ever possessing 'his book' because he didn't want to run the risk of becoming 'an imitator, willingly or not'. Petrarch goes on to admit that this stance was the product of youthful pride and arrogance. If one ever should find anything in his own work that seems similar to that 'of him or of anyone else', Boccaccio needs to understand that it will simply be because of chance or because of similar talents.

In any case, things had now changed, as Petrarch explained: 'Today, all of these worries are far behind me. Now that I have departed and have put aside that fear by which I was held back, I welcome with my whole mind all others and him above all.'[7] Note that Petrarch does not specify whom precisely he welcomes. He means 'poets' or 'writers', but he cannot even bring himself to say that much. Again, Dante is reduced to 'him'. The more important factor in the letter at this point is Petrarch's posture. Distantly echoing 1 Corinthians ('When I became a man, I put away childish things,' 1 Cor. 13:11), Petrarch is suggesting that he has reached a new phase, one that has to do, in many if not most respects, with language. Earlier in the letter, when Petrarch had been explaining away his youthful decision never to acquire Dante's work for fear of unwittingly imitating it, he said about the vernacular that, at that point in his life, he considered 'nothing more elegant' and that he had not yet come to 'aspire to higher matters'.[8] What Petrarch is saying, in other words, is that now, in his full maturity, he has devoted himself to Latin: to his scholarly projects in prose and, in poetry, to his *Africa*. There is a real sense in which that was true, on the surface. But surfaces can be deceiving. For even as Petrarch continued his work in Latin in the latter part of his life, he also devoted great effort to his two monuments in the vernacular: his *Canzoniere* and his *Triumphs*.

Before we arrive at those and other of Petrarch's late-in-life efforts, however, a look at the second of the three letters under examination is warranted. For it is in this epistle that Petrarch sets forth his ideas on imitation, which is to say on how and to what extent one should use and imitate respected ancient models. And the letter points to something else that is unique and interesting about Petrarch's world and the culture of reading and writing that he inhabited. This letter was precipitated by Petrarch's desire to have Boccaccio

change a few lines in manuscripts of poetry which Petrarch
had given to him – to make sure, in other words, that Boccaccio
had the most up-to-date version of one of Petrarch's own
writings.

As to reading and writing: we need always to keep in the
front of our minds how different the world of publication
was in Petrarch's day. For this, in fact, is what he is doing:
'publishing', in the sense of 'making public' to the audiences
that mattered and counted to him. The poetry in question is
known as the '*Bucolicum carmen*', or 'Bucolics', a title that echoes and imitates one of the titles by which people knew
Virgil's *Eclogues*, those foundational pastoral poems set in sylvan locations and interwoven, sometimes implicitly, sometimes
explicitly, with political themes. Petrarch composed twelve of
these and, as he did, he would share them as they evolved with
trusted friends and readers. In this case he had shared one
with Boccaccio, who read it quickly and intensely and took a
copy with him as he departed. But then, after Boccaccio had
left, Petrarch shared the same poem with another friend who,
as it happens, was a slower reader. That slower reading process revealed that Petrarch had included in the language of
his poem some inadvertent but exact similarities, in one
case to the language of Virgil, in another to that of Ovid. So
Petrarch eventually asks Boccaccio, at the very end of what is
in truth a long letter, to change those two lines in the copy
that Boccaccio possessed. The point – with respect to reading, writing, and 'publication' – is that Boccaccio would be
likely to share Petrarch's often eagerly awaited works with
his own social and intellectual circles. Petrarch would have
expected this to occur. So he wanted to make sure that

Boccaccio had the most up-to-date version. What we observe is that publication was complete (to speak somewhat flippantly) only when changes could no longer be made – in other words, when an author was dead.

Beyond early publication practices and how Petrarch framed his writing, this letter also affords a glimpse into how Petrarch related to certain ancient authors. This relation has to do primarily with reading and, more specifically, with styles of reading. Petrarch tells Boccaccio that there are certain authors that he has read 'intensely and quickly, with no delays at all except as one would in foreign territory'.[9] He names four authors (Ennius, Plautus, Martianus Capella and Apuleius), explaining that, in those cases, what he has read sticks out so clearly in his mind that it is as if they sit 'in the vestibule of my memory'.[10] What he means is that, if he comes upon a passage from one of those authors, he can recognize it clearly. He realizes it is written by another author and consequently that is not his own work.

Not so in the case of certain other authors. Here (in a passage we have encountered before) Petrarch mentions Virgil, Horace, Boethius and Cicero:

> I read them not once but a thousand times; I did not run by them but lay down beside them; I brooded over them with every effort of my intelligence. I ate in the morning what I would digest in the evening; I imbibed as a boy what I would ruminate on as an older man.[11]

Already we see that Petrarch is projecting an intimacy with certain key ancient authors, intensified by the physical metaphors with which he packs his description. What he goes on to say is even more striking:

> I have ingested these things in such an intimate way that they have become fixed not only in my memory but in my marrow, having become as one with my own intellect. The result is that, even if I never read them again for the rest of my life, they would certainly stick, having taken deep root in the deepest part of my spirit. Meanwhile, however, I might very well forget the author, since because of long use and continual possession, it is as if I had written those things down and considered them my own, and, besieged as I am by such a great crowd of these sorts of things, I don't remember with certainty whose they are or even that they are not my own.[12]

The language here is noteworthy and, if it sounds a bit awkward in English it is also, if not awkward, at least heavily freighted in Latin. Petrarch simply refers to what he has read repeatedly as 'these things' (using the pronoun *haec* in Latin), so that what were once individual texts by individual authors become, instead, something like prime matter, ready to be deployed and converted into different forms by the hand of the new author, Petrarch. Or, more prosaically and in line with Petrarch's own metaphors, these individual texts become like food that has been digested, a source of energy that fuels one's daily endeavours.

Petrarch also signals a sense of being walled in or trapped by his reading, when he says that he is 'besieged by a great crowd of these sorts of things'. The word he uses in Latin for 'besieged' is *obsessus*, whose primary meaning is indeed military in orientation, signalling 'blockades', 'sieges' and 'taking possession', as you would of a town in war. In Petrarch's usage, the word also has something of the English resonance as well: 'obsession'. Surrounded (willingly of course) by great and venerated authors as he is, Petrarch must also seek distinction; he must find a way to delineate his own persona. It is crucial that Boccaccio understands what is at stake: 'I call to witness Apollo, the singularly born son of Jove, and the true God of wisdom, Christ: I have never been eager to prey on anyone, and just as I have always abstained from the spoils of other people's estates, so too have I abstained from other people's creative talents.'[13] Apollo and Christ are in the same sentence: a pair whose members are graded in importance and who together keep watch over knowledge and truth. With the backing of both, Petrarch makes sure that Boccaccio knows that Petrarch's work is Petrarch's own. Any similarities are inadvertent or the result of similar intelligences producing similar results. After all, 'I confess that I wish to adorn my life, but not my style, with what others have said and advised.'[14]

Finally, he comes to the end of the letter and to his request that Boccaccio change the passages in question. After the request, simple enough, he concludes by asking Boccaccio for help: 'should you notice more such things' – meaning, more passages in which Petrarch had inadvertently used the work of others too closely – 'correct them according to your own judgment or advise me of them in a friendly fashion. Indeed, nothing would be more welcome in my eyes than if you or

anyone at all who is a friend would censure me with a spirit
that is friendly, free, and undaunted.'[15] Petrarch is ready with
a 'most equitable spirit' to accept such corrections, not only,
in fact, from people who are friends but even from 'the bark-
ing of rivals, provided that I can glimpse any spark at all of
truth amidst the shadows of hatred. Live happily, mindful of
me, and be well.'[16] As much as Petrarch framed his relationship with Boccaccio as that of master to pupil, it is clear that
he sought the younger Boccaccio's approval, even as he trusted
Boccaccio ever more with curating and safeguarding his
reputation.

Petrarch collected his letters, and the final set is known
as the *Res seniles*, or *Matters of Old Age*. Among these letters is one
to Boccaccio written in 1364. In it their relationship comes
into play, we see the emergence of what will become the
canon of early Italian literature, and more information about
the world of reading and writing comes to the fore. For good
measure, Petrarch also throws in some testy criticism of the
modern age, the tenor of which had 'legs', as it were, and
would reappear in the following century.

At the outset it is obvious that Petrarch believes they are
in what may seem sensitive territory, as he signals that he has
a specific concern he wishes to raise. Petrarch first stresses
that nothing is closer to his own spirit than Boccaccio's and
that he considers the two of them to be 'one spirit in two bodies'.[17] Petrarch then moves, in a winding fashion, as he tends
to do, to his concern, by talking about poetry in a way that
(again, as earlier) tells us a lot about how written work circulated. He tells Boccaccio that he has been practically under
siege by crowds of 'men who, though they possess no great

talent, do instead possess great memories, diligence and, in truth, audacity, as they frequent the halls of kings and other powerful people.'[18] 'Fitted out in other people's poetry', they recite things *materno charactere* – in the mother tongue, essentially – for pay.[19] These wandering reciters of poetry come to Petrarch, begging from him some lines of poetry that they then might recite. Sometimes he is so sick of them that he cannot accede to their requests, whereas at other times he feels pity and gives them a little something so that they can earn enough to stay fed.

Then he arrives at the real point he wanted to make. On one occasion, some of these wandering reciters of poetry related something exceedingly strange, reporting (Petrarch is addressing Boccaccio) 'that you had burned whatsoever you possessed of your own vernacular poems'.[20] Stunned as Petrarch was to hear this news, he asked the visitors why Boccaccio would have done this. Though most were silent, one responded, to the effect that (again, Petrarch is addressing Boccaccio) 'you wanted to revise all those things that had slipped out of your hands when you were young, now that you had reached a more mature and solid old age'.[21] Petrarch's befuddlement only increased when he heard more on this topic from 'our friend Donato' (Donato Albanzani, a mutual friend of the two men), who gave Petrarch more of the context for Boccaccio's actions. Petrarch says:

> Donato told me that you, when young and extraordinarily devoted to the vernacular [Tuscan] style, dedicated a great deal of effort and time to it, until in the course of your efforts you came upon my own

youthful compositions in that genre. From that point on your desire to write cooled. And you were not content simply to stop writing similar things going forward. No, instead you declared your hatred for the things you had already completed and you burned them all with the intention of destroying them rather than of revising them. And so you not only would despoil yourself but also posterity of the fruits of your labour in this regard, for no other reason than that you thought them unequal to my own.[22]

So now we have it: it was envy and insecurity that had moved Boccaccio to burn his work, and the object of his envy was none other than Petrarch himself. Petrarch exclaims: 'What an unworthy hatred! What an undeserved fire!'[23]

It is worth noting that something like what is described probably happened in reality: a slightly younger poet, Boccaccio, enthused by Tuscan poetry (and inspired of course by Dante who, again, goes unnamed in this letter of Petrarch's), would have given every youthful effort to make his mark, only to be caught up short when confronted with Petrarch's emerging lyricism. Their relationship comes to the fore of course, as does consciousness of their own relative places in an evolving ranking of Italian poets. Indeed, it is to this latter aspect that Petrarch turns next, adopting the persona of the wise older mentor willing to show tough love to his younger contemporary. And tough love it is, as Petrarch says he is uncertain as to whether Boccaccio, in his poetry-burning episode, was manifesting 'humility of the sort that reflects a contempt of oneself, or the pride of one who raises himself above others'.[24] Petrarch then gets in Boccaccio's head a bit, having just raised that question of humility versus pride: 'You judge your own spirit for yourself. I will muddle along taking the way of conjecture, as I am accustomed to do when I speak with you.'[25] What follows is an extraordinary Petrarchan mix: there are humility and pride on Petrarch's own part, alpha-male subordination of a beloved associate and, most importantly, an expression of Petrarch's consciousness of his own, Dante's, and Boccaccio's relative places in an emerging Italian literary history.

After citations of a few examples of ancient writers who worried overmuch about rankings, Petrarch says what he feels: 'I fear that your so noteworthy "humility" is actually pride.'[26] He then goes on:

> So let us say that I am in fact placed ahead of you (would that I could be your equal!) and that also ahead of you is that leader of our vernacular eloquence; would it really bother you so much to be preceded by one or two people (your fellow citizens at that) or, to put it another way, to be preceded by really very few people?[27]

We can note that Petrarch establishes a ranking. 'That leader of our vernacular eloquence' is Dante. Petrarch comes in second, and Boccaccio is third. There is a bit of an attempt to assuage what might be Boccaccio's hurt feelings ('would that I could be your equal'), but the import is clear. In the realm of the vernacular, in any case, Boccaccio comes in third.

Most noteworthy about all this is that in Petrarch's somewhat rambling set of statements, we see the first real iteration

17 Andrea del Castagno, *Dante Alighieri*, c. 1450, detached fresco transferred to canvas.

of the founding canon of Italian literature, in a ranking that
has persisted: Dante, Petrarch, Boccaccio, in that order and
not only chronologically but in terms of relative place. Soon
thereafter proud Florentines would refer to that grouping as
the *tre corone* or the 'three crowns' of Florence.[28] As such, the
three authors became not only a source of pride for the city
but also, eventually, the bedrock of the Italian language, when,
almost two centuries thereafter, thinkers looked towards
canonical models of how to use the Tuscan language (illus.
17, 18, 19).

All of that was far off in Petrarch's day. More immediately
(and to return to his letter) he wants to find a way to have
Boccaccio comfortable at a subordinate rank. Petrarch explains
that it can actually be a stimulus to great achievement if one
sits at a rank lower than first: 'jealousy stimulates both lovers
and scholars, since without a rival love languishes, and without an emulator, virtue grows numb.'[29] The word 'emulator'
is significant. The Latin word is *aemulus*, directly related to
the Latin word *aemulatio*, or 'emulation' most literally. But it
is a capacious word that encompasses a number of different
meanings all at once: imitation, competition, striving, rivalry.
Petrarch is speaking in this instance about poets who are
relative contemporaries. But eventually the idea of *aemulatio*,
which we can define as 'rivalrous imitation', served as a concept
gesturing towards what many Renaissance thinkers believed
about Graeco-Roman antiquity: that it must be imitated but
imitated in a critical fashion. You needed to see yourself as
within the same competitive universe as the ancients and –
eventually – able to surpass them. Like so much else involving
Petrarch, he can be seen as setting that tendency to want to

surpass the ancients in motion, even if he never fully arrived at that point.

As to the rest of the letter, after more comments about rankings and about the need for Boccaccio to be satisfied with his position, Petrarch offers Boccaccio his real recommendation: 'So spare the flames and take pity on your poetry.'[30] Move on, in other words, and let your poetry alone, however third-rank it may be. Petrarch then makes a transition that sheds more light on his view of himself vis-à-vis the ancients, his sense of what the vernacular was all about and his perception that the vernacular was far more difficult to control. He admits to Boccaccio that he too had once thought to burn his youthful Italian poetry and in fact would have done so if it were not for the fact that his poetry was by that point 'so well known that it was beyond my control'.[31] Petrarch then goes on in a passage that is worth extended quotation:

> Now it is true that at one time I had indeed had an intention contrary to my current one, hoping to devote most of my time to this enterprise of writing in the vernacular. The reason is that it seemed to me that both of the two more elevated styles of Latin [prose and poetry] had been cultivated to such an extent and by such great geniuses of antiquity that nothing significant could be added, either by me or by anyone else. On the other hand, the vernacular, having been but recently discovered and still quite rustic owing to recent ravagers and to the fact that few have cultivated it, seemed capable of ornament and augmentation.[32]

18 Andrea del Castagno, *Francesco Petrarca, c.* 1450, detached fresco transferred to canvas.

19 Andrea del Castagno, *Giovanni Boccaccio*, c. 1450, detached fresco transferred to canvas.

Here, Petrarch notes that, as a younger man under the spell of antiquity, he became overwhelmed by the idea of being able to write anything in Latin, whether poetry or prose, that could reach the heights to which the ancients had ascended. This pressure weighed on him to such an extent that he turned to the vernacular. Again, there is a kind of passive aggression towards Dante, when Petrarch says that the vernacular was only 'recently discovered and still quite rustic', since Dante's *Comedy* had achieved almost instant fame.

Then Petrarch moves to a rather curious and ambiguous description of what he did next:

> Urged on by the stimuli of youth, I had begun a great work in that genre, and I had laid down the foundations of the edifice along with the plaster, stone, and wood. But then when I looked at our own age, the mother of pride and indolence, I began with some bitterness to note how great was the 'genius' of those who tossed those things around, how 'beautiful' was their style of speaking. The result is that you would say writings are not recited but ripped apart.[33]

Much needs deciphering here. First, 'a great work in that genre'. What work? What genre? The 'great work' in question might be his *Triumphs*, which we will get to know in greater detail later. Or it might very well be his *Rerum vulgarium fragmenta*, as he titled it in Latin – his 'Fragments of Things in the Vernacular' – which is more popularly known in Italian as his *Canzoniere*, in other words the Italian lyric poetry by which he is best known today. Either way, his implication to

Boccaccio is that it was a project he had begun but that he has now, as an older man, abandoned. Youth was for the vernacular, maturity for Latin. Love and song are for the young, philosophy and religion for those who are older and wiser.

Why, precisely, he made this transition is a question with deeper resonances. In fact, we might say that Petrarch chose, as he carefully fashioned his image, to have it known that he made a transition, rather than actually making one. For the truth is that he kept working on his vernacular poetry throughout his life, keeping the flame alive, if hidden, in the hope that he might one day emerge as a vernacular poet of lasting fame. The same letter also points to a more immediate reason why Petrarch came to mistrust the vernacular. Simply put, vernacular poetry was memorized and sung in public contexts. And whenever oral poetic performance is in play, it means that those doing the reciting are the ones delivering what was once only on the page. This problematic admixture of oral and written is that to which Petrarch is referring, with evident sarcasm, when he signals 'those who tossed those things around' – 'things' being written works – and then simultaneously indicts their 'beautiful' style of speaking. What was at issue for Petrarch, most obviously, was control over his writing. The problem, as he brings into relief, is that professional poetry-reciters worked in such a way that 'writings' (Petrarch uses the Latin word *scripta*, meaning simply 'things written down') are 'not recited but ripped apart'. For ripped apart, he uses the Latin *discerpi*, which is a word connoting violence, along the lines of dismemberment.

What is clear is that Petrarch had a deep emotional connection not only to his writing broadly conceived, but to his writing as writing, which is to say the specific words, in the specific sequence that he himself put on a page, either directly or through a professional scribe whom he supervised. So in one respect, his self-styled transition away from the vernacular and towards Latin was about control: there would be fewer people in a position to understand Latin, and, given that it was a secondary language for all who used it, it was less likely to be recited in public squares or at the courts of people who could sponsor the recital of poetry.

What is less clear is how accurately this letter captures what was really going on in Petrarch's tormented psychology. He goes on to evince nothing short of disgust:

> Having heard this once, then again, then quite often, and thinking it over ever more intensely, I finally came to the realization that, by building on soft mud and unsteady sand, I would be wasting time and that I, along with my work, would be torn apart at the hands of the crowd.[34]

Again, one senses Petrarch's strong identification of self and work, as well as a gnawing fear of losing unity, of being 'torn apart'. We observe Petrarch's particular combination of high self-regard, a concern for cultivating friendship (as he is doing in this letter to Boccaccio), and misanthropy – his hatred for the 'crowd', meaning those who would enjoy vernacular poetry but not be sufficiently scrupulous about reproducing it exactly as its author intended (illus. 20). It is also apparent that this outburst is a performance, in a sense. Petrarch must have realized that poetry in his day was as oral as it was written and that it was inevitable and, indeed, desirable that poetry be on people's lips.

Petrarch goes on to tell Boccaccio that, like someone who saw a snake in the road, he changed course and 'took another road, one that was straighter and higher', even as he realized that his youthful vernacular poetry – 'those things that were scattered and short' – was by now, in effect, common property. He will try, however, not to allow them to be 'torn apart'.[35] This latter statement, indicating that he will indeed be paying at least some attention to his vernacular poetry, signals obliquely that he will keep editing and revising that very poetry without, however, making much public fuss about the process.

By now, however, Petrarch's ire has been raised, and he is ready to rail against everything in his era that bothers him. It is not just that the ignorance of the unlearned is disturbing. His larger concern is with 'those who call themselves learned . . . who beyond other absurdities add the greatest pride to the lowest ignorance – a hateful thing'.[36] Before Petrarch continues with this censure of the so-called learned of his day, he appears to condemn everything: 'Oh, what an inglorious age: you look down on antiquity, your mother and the discoverer of all the noble arts and then dare not only to put yourself on the same level but also to rank yourself higher!'[37] The whole thing is bad, bottom to top: the common people ('those feces of men'), military leaders ('who go to war as if they are going to a wedding' and care more about opulent feasts than they do about winning battles) and the political class (who care more about the symbols of rule – 'gold and purple' – than they do about governing in an honourable way). Yet all of these groups, bad as they are, at least have the

20 Frontispiece by Francesco di Antonio del Chierico that depicts Petrarch writing (or sleeping?) in his study, from a copy of Petrarch's *Rime; Trionfi* from *c.* 1470.

excuse that they are not very highly educated. 'But what, I ask, will excuse learned men who, though they must not be unaware of the ancients, still languish in that very same blindness of their opinions?' In case Boccaccio wasn't getting the tone, Petrarch goes on: 'Understand, my good friend, that I am angry when I say these things and that I do so in a bitter and irritated way.'[38]

The real problem has to do with both the form and, Petrarch asserts, the content of what some contemporaries consider the highest form of learning. This style of cultural critique lasted perdurably throughout the Renaissance. While there has never been a historical era without its share of ill-tempered critics, Petrarch can be said to have inaugurated this specific variety of criticism: one that links eloquence with substance and, more specifically, the acquisition of knowledge with religious piety. The basic point is that institutionalized forms of creating and diffusing knowledge are not getting at what is really important:

> These days, little dialecticians, who are not so much ignorant as crazy, are rising up like a black battle-line of ants and bursting out, as if from the dark recesses of some kind of pocked oak tree, and ruining all the arable land of higher learning as they do so. These characters condemn Plato and Aristotle and laugh at Socrates and Pythagoras. And – good God! – they do all this with aid of such incompetent leaders![39]

To a modern reader this phraseology might seem obscure. Petrarch is referring to contemporary intellectuals who devote most of their time to 'dialectic', or what we know as logic. He refuses to identify the people he has in mind ('I don't want to name people whose deeds don't deserve it'), but his problem is that these unnamed thinkers have dived so deep into the murky sea of hyper-specialization that they are unable to focus on what really matters: living a good, ethical life that reflects Christian predispositions. The fact that many of these thinkers found themselves on theology faculties of universities was even worse, for their research interests threatened to corrupt society from inside.

We can delve deeper into what all of this meant by following Petrarch and his conversation with Boccaccio as it winds to an end. Petrarch details a specific episode in a way that is as colourful as it is arresting. He begins by saying that it has become habitual among this new, arrogant and odious type of thinker to denigrate the ancient church fathers, legends like Ambrose, Augustine and Jerome, with tacit gestures or words that smack of impiety. '"Augustine", they say, "saw much but knew little".'[40] Petrarch goes on: 'Not long ago, one of these men arrived in my library.' This thinker (again, unnamed) was 'one of those who philosophizes in the "modern" manner, who think they have achieved nothing if they haven't barked something against Christ and against Christ's heavenly doctrine'.[41] So the picture Petrarch is drawing in some obvious respects fits a pattern: this person was arrogant, seemingly doing intellectual work related to Christianity, but in so doing was actually going against the most important Christian principles.

Petrarch then brought forwards 'some passage from a sacred work', and upon hearing it his guest, 'spewing rabid rage and, aided by anger and contempt, distorting his face into an expression even uglier than it was by nature, said: "Take your little doctors of the Church. For my part, I have someone whom I follow and something in which I believe."[42] As it happens, part of that phrase is a slightly altered quotation of scripture, so Petrarch in his response quotes some scripture of his own.[43] But the important point is that this young thinker seemed overtly to show disrespect for the 'doctors' of the church – in other words the very same sorts of church fathers (Augustine, Ambrose, and so on) whose holy eloquence Petrarch was ever prepared to defend.

Finally, things rise to such a pitch that the arrogant guest says something unpardonable. Addressing Petrarch, he said:

'You – go ahead and be a good Christian. For my part I believe none of those things. Your Paul, your Augustine, indeed all those about whom you preach: they were the wordiest of men. If only you could bear Avveroes. Then you would see how much greater he is than these triflers of yours.'[44]

This statement pushed Petrarch over the edge. He responded in this fashion: 'This is an old question between me and other heretics like you. So get yourself and your heresy out of here, never to return!' Adding a little physical flair to the description, Petrarch then informs Boccaccio: 'I grabbed him by his coat and threw him out, in a way that was more insolent than my usual custom, if not more than his.'[45]

Unpacking this episode allows us to understand something of Petrarch's mindset and his effects on the Renaissance after him. The terms involved and Petrarch's evident emotion can be difficult to understand today. Saints Paul and Augustine are familiar enough. Paul was the chief evangelist of the then new offshoot of Judaism that became Christianity, whose letters became touchstones in the history of Christianity and the formation of Christian scripture. His letter to the Romans, which preached personal humility in the face of an omniscient, omnipotent God, served as a great inspiration to Augustine (354–430 CE), whose *Confessions* were so meaningful to Petrarch.

Yet Averroes is a lesser-known figure, somewhat surprisingly so, given his impact on medieval thought. Active for almost the whole length of the twelfth century, Averroes was a Spanish Muslim who wrote in Arabic. He revered the ancient Greek thinker Aristotle, whose works had served as the foundation for medieval Islamic thought. When Aristotle's works were translated into Latin in the twelfth and thirteenth centuries, sometimes from the original Greek, sometimes from Arabic intermediaries, Averroes' commentaries on those works also made their way into Latin. Averroes' commentaries thus became part of how Aristotle was read and understood in the West, so much so that Averroes became known as 'the commentator' (Dante in the fourth canto of his *Inferno* refers to Averroes as 'the one who wrote the great commentary').[46] In thirteenth-century Western Europe, Aristotle became the central thinker, and his writings served as the key works around which debate turned. Academic curricula emerged around Aristotle's works, and Europe's leading thinkers laboured intensively, both to understand Aristotle and, when possible, to harmonize his thought with Christianity. Averroes and his brilliant commentaries represented another way in, as it were, another arrow in the interpretive quiver Western thinkers employed to decipher Aristotelian difficulties.

And difficulties there were. One of these, concerning the human soul, can serve as an example. Aristotle believed that the human soul was what he called the final actuality of a person. What he meant by this was that the soul was akin to the form of a person. We might think of this as a 'pattern' of sorts but, importantly, not as a pre-existing pattern or one that had a separate existence from the actual, physical person.[47] Aristotle believed that material things had a real existence only when they represented a unity of matter and form. So, when it came to the human person, he was at best ambiguous as to whether anything of an individual might survive physical death. At worst, Aristotle seemed to suggest that, when a person physically died, that person's soul died along with him. But he was indefinite and could be read both ways.

For medieval Christians, this ambiguity represented a problem of great moment. Christians held, of course, that the individual soul was immortal, which is to say that something formally distinct of the individual human person survived physical death. Whatever it was that Aristotle said, that was not it. Adding Averroes into the equation complicated matters even more.

One of the key problems was one of knowledge. Aristotle said that when we know things about the world, we know them first of all based on our physical sense impressions, meaning simply this: you cannot know something unless your senses are involved, at least at first. But then there was another level, which involved processing information in which the intellect was involved. But whose intellect? Aristotle said that there was also a larger intellect in the universe, and, tantalizingly, he had linked individual human acts of intellection to that larger intellect.[48] Averroes in his interpretation then raised the stakes, linking Aristotle's larger, supra-human intellect to humanity itself and suggesting that, when human beings died, that part of their soul that engaged in activity of the intellect became unified with the larger universal intellect. On the one hand, this interpretation served to buttress the idea that there was something immortal about the human soul. On the other, it suggested that what was individual about the human person would no longer exist after death, instead being absorbed into a unified, larger, universal intellect. The idea that there could be individual rewards and punishments after death would thus be off the table.

This was one of many positions that Averroes had taken in his massive commentaries on Aristotle's works. As universities grew in the thirteenth century and thinkers dived ever more deeply into Aristotle's works, tensions arose as Christian leaders realized that some of Aristotle's positions were difficult if not impossible to reconcile with Christian orthodoxy, and that certain Averroistic positions were simply heretical.

The volume of the discussion rose to such an extent that in 1277 the bishop of Paris issued a condemnation that forbade the teaching and discussion of 219 statements that had become objects of lively enquiry among students and faculty at the University of Paris, Europe's most important centre at the time for the study of theology.[49] Tellingly, one of the condemned propositions was that 'the intellect is one for all men'; there were other Averroistic ideas that had become controversial as well. The paradox was that Averroes was seen by many theologians struggling to understand Aristotle as a great interpreter and, importantly, as *au courant*: using Averroes could be seen, in other words, as new and exciting. By Petrarch's day – to close this parenthesis – Averroes could be seen alternately as either a kind of bogeyman (a heretical Islamic thinker corrupting Christianity), or as a representative of some of the newest and most exciting scholarship around.

So when Petrarch reports his encounter with the arrogant Averroist philosopher to Boccaccio, we hear echoes of that history. We can also observe that what Petrarch says foreshadows one type of criticism that will run throughout the Italian Renaissance after him and that can, indeed, be traced to him as a point of origin. This line of cultural critique suggests, implicitly and explicitly, that institutionalized forms of knowledge creation are not doing the job they should be doing. Although Petrarch does not say it in those terms in his letters to Boccaccio, it is clear that the Averroes-influenced philosopher who has incited Petrarch is from the university world.

This anti-institutional bent emerges in other works of Petrarch, as we shall see. For now, it is enough to say that in his letters to Boccaccio, we witness an ageing Petrarch, who complains about the world in which he finds himself. He is increasingly concerned with his reputation, with where he sits relative to Dante, and with precisely what sort of connection with the ancient world his own work might have. Petrarch the 'wanderer' is present in those letters, skipping as he does from topic to topic, across the vast terrain that his work in both Latin and the vernacular represented. As we turn to the final years of Petrarch's life, it is appropriate to see how his wanderer's mentality played itself out in his work.

SIX

Endings

FTER 1353, PETRARCH REMAINED tied firmly to Italy for the rest of his life, though his wanderer's spirit remained. Throughout that time, he accepted patronage from a number of different rulers and cities. From 1353 until 1361, he was mostly in Milan, at the court of the powerful Visconti family, even serving once as their ambassador to the Holy Roman Emperor Charles IV, who was based in Prague.

It is telling that Petrarch's first major stint in Italy was in Milan among the Visconti. The Visconti ruled Milan as a despotism, meaning that Milan functioned under one-man (and one-family) rule. This mode of governance was common in late medieval Italy, and Petrarch would go on to accept patronage from other such states and rulers. Yet he was always proud to consider himself a Florentine by origin. Florence by contrast was a republic, a state in which those who had gained the right of citizenship could and did participate actively in governance. It is worth bringing up these different forms of government and Petrarch's participation in them, if for no other reason than to highlight that Petrarch was not really interested in the practicalities of politics. He was interested, instead, in himself, following patronage wherever it led, spurning (after his lengthy infatuation with the figure of Cola di Rienzo) detailed involvement in politics, except when required by his patrons. The year 1361 saw Petrarch move to Venice, after there was a new outbreak of plague in Milan, and then from 1367 on he received patronage from the Carrara family in Padua. In 1370 he acquired a country house in Arquà, outside of Padua, where he spent most of the rest of his time until 1374, the year of his death.

During this last, 'Italian' period of his life, Petrarch continued to focus on his work. Though in his letters to Boccaccio and indeed in his famous 'Letter to Posterity', Petrarch said (perhaps a bit too loudly) that his focus had turned from Italian to Latin and from poetry to philosophy, his Italian poetry remained an object of constant concern.

For one thing, he never stopped working on the *Canzoniere*, his collection of Italian poems that he referred to as 'Fragments of Things in the Vernacular'. We have seen how Petrarch memorialized and allegorized his love for Laura (in the poem '*Voglia mi sprona*'), embraced political themes (in '*Spirto gentil*'), and even made a statement about Italy as such, imagining it as exiles often do as more than just a collection of city-states but as a possible political unity (in '*Italia mia*'). The *Canzoniere* is a masterpiece, and as such, it possesses endless possibilities for interpretation.

We see Petrarch struggling to make his decision to leave Provence in one of the poems, likely written in the late 1340s and revealing as ever his deep connection to Laura and to the environment in which he first saw her. Titled '*A la dolce ombra delle belle frondi*' – 'In the Sweet Shade of the Beautiful Foliage' – it begins with Petrarch looking back to a time when he saw and desired this tree of great beauty: 'The world never saw such elegant branches, nor did the wind ever move such green foliage as were shown to me in those early days.'[1] Laura merges with the landscape of southern France, as Petrarch idealized and imagined it, her hair like the foliage (youthful and fresh), her body like the elegant limbs of the tree. Petrarch says he once felt protected by the 'laurel', which 'defended him back then from the sky'.[2] But as time passed he came to realize how many other 'woods, stones, country-sides, rivers, and hills' had been created.[3] The poet is now in a position to change: 'Other love, other foliage and other light, another way of getting to heaven over other hills, do I seek – for it is the time to do so – and other branches too.'[4] His own psychology ever in the front of his mind, Petrarch opens the door, here and elsewhere, into his struggles and into the chronology of his life.

Elsewhere he is more direct. He wrote a series of poems in the *Canzoniere* that attacked the morality of the papal court at Avignon. In one he voiced his hope that a 'flame from heaven might rain down on your tresses', thus personifying the Church as the 'great whore', spoken of in the Book of Revelation.[5] The Church was guilty of 'making itself rich and great by impoverishing others' and was a 'nest of betrayals' where everything bad in the world was bred.[6] He goes on to accuse the Church of being a 'slave of wine, of beds, of food', a place in which every kind of debauchery finds a home, a place where 'throughout your rooms young girls and old men carry out their affairs'.[7] He ends the poem by saying: 'live, then, so that your stench reaches God.'[8]

It might surprise a modern reader to hear Petrarch, in some respects the most religious of men, hurling this sort of reprobation at the Catholic Church, Christianity's central organ in the Middle Ages. And it was not only in his poetry that he expressed these sorts of opinions. He wrote a whole series of anonymous Latin letters (called the 'Letters Without a Name') denouncing the morality of the Church and equating Avignon with Babylon, a city that in the Book of Revelation was described as (among other things) a prostitute drunk on the blood of saints – an equation he employed in the poem just quoted.[9] Why the vehemence? One reason is that, whenever people are close to the inner workings of an institution, they see details to which outsiders are not privy. The Church had emerged, by the fourteenth century, as a political power in ways that are hard to understand today. It had developed a bureaucracy analogous to those in other late medieval states, and in its inner workings it behaved a lot like a politically active state.

Yet for Petrarch (and, in truth, for many others like him) the Church seemed to have gone too far down that road. Those who took this view believed that the Church had strayed from its true mission: promoting the Christian message of humility, faith in Christ and serving others. Petrarch's vehement poem suggests not only that the Church has become overly wealthy, but that it has done so at the expense of others. At the heart there is moral rot, with 'old men' (he means, of course, senior clerics) engaging in disgraceful affairs with young girls. Couching his language as he does in references to the Book of Revelation – also called the Book of the Apocalypse – Petrarch is hinting obliquely that he believes that the end times are, if not at hand, possibly imminent. As Europe suffered a devastating plague that wiped out between a third and half of its population, these beliefs would have only grown in intensity.

Petrarch's disapproval of the current, contemporary Church should not be understood as a critique of Christianity. All of his writing, especially during the final period of his life, reflected a deeply Christian sensibility, which can be glimpsed from the rest of his work, and especially from three texts he worked on in the last part of his life: his *Remedies of Fortune Fair and Foul*, his invective *On his Own Ignorance and That of Many Others* and his *Triumph of Eternity*.

The *Remedies of Fortune Fair and Foul* (*De remediis utriusque fortunae* in Latin) is a work of its time and place, one that, though it has limited appeal today, allows us an important glimpse into Petrarch's world. It has the distinction of being one of the only larger works he wrote that he completed in an expeditious and focused way. A series of 254 short Latin dialogues, the *Remedies* occupied much of Petrarch's time between 1354 and 1357, when he was in Milan at the service of the Visconti. The *Remedies* were popular in their day: we possess over 250 manuscript copies of the text. Tellingly, however, its popularity dropped off in the era of printing with moveable type, which took off in the 1450s, as the relative paucity of early printed editions attests.[10] What this tells us was that the *Remedies* spoke to its time and place, but not so much to later generations.

Broadly speaking, we can classify the *Remedies* as a specimen of wisdom literature with a philosophical leaning towards Stoicism. As a text it is divided into two books, the first concerning good fortune and how to deal with it (containing 122 dialogues), the second on bad fortune (containing the remaining 132 dialogues). Noteworthy regarding the dialogues that make up the *Remedies* are the interlocutors: Joy, Hope, Fear, Despair and Reason. They are all 'personifications', which is to say that they are personalized representations of general qualities (illus. 21). The first four represent the soul's passions, those qualities of a person's soul that can be swayed by emotion, that oscillate – sometimes wildly – and that, if not moderated, can lead to unhappiness. Reason, on the other hand, can serve as that necessary moderating force.

The easiest way to understand what Petrarch is up to is to take a look at one of these dialogues, an early one in the first book, called 'I Was Born in a Glorious Homeland'. In it, the two interlocutors are Joy and Reason, and it is precisely that moderating role that Reason plays.[11] The interlocutor Joy begins with a simple statement, and their first exchange is concise, simple and revealing.

Joy: 'I was born in a glorious homeland.'
  Reason: 'You will have all the more trouble when the light is upon you. The smaller stars shine only at night, and Bootes (the herdsman), as well as Lucifer (the morning star) seem dim in the light of the sun's rays.'
  Joy: 'I am a citizen of a most famous homeland.'
  Reason: 'This is a good thing, provided that you are a friend of virtue and an enemy of vice. The former [citizenship], depends on fortune, whereas the latter [being a friend of virtue and enemy of vice] depends on you.'
  Joy: 'My homeland is fortunate and noble.'

Reason: 'One should see what sort of nobility this is. For nobility emerges from the number of inhabitants one finds there, the abundance of wealth, the fertility of its land, its geographic situation, healthful air, pure springs, proximity to the sea, safe harbors, and fortunately placed rivers . . . You say that a land is good when you see good horses born there, big fat cows, tender goats, and fruits rich with juice. But whether there are good men? About this you certainly neither ask nor think it worthy of consideration – O, what outstanding judges you are! For indeed, the highest praise of a homeland is this alone: the virtue of its citizens.'[12]

We recall Petrarch's *Secret*, where he had wrestled with his own indecision and perceived weaknesses in private. Even from this short opening section of 'I Was Born in a Glorious

21 Detail of a manuscript illumination depicting the wheel of fortune, from the first page of a 14th-century copy of Petrarch's *De Remediis utriusque fortunae*.

Homeland', we can see that Petrarch offers here a public, outward-facing counterpart to that very same sort of mental and spiritual exercise that he had deployed so well (if only for himself) in the *Secret*. In this case, the central concern is the sort of 'homeland' whence one hails and how one should feel about one's origin. The word translated here as 'homeland' is the Latin *patria*. In English it could also be translated as 'fatherland' or 'country', though that latter word, in current English usage, tends to imply a much larger unit than that to which Petrarch here refers. He is talking about city-states in the late medieval world, small enough usually that one could walk across them but often big enough power players that they could wage war, possess the equivalent of foreign policies and serve as major political actors.

'Joy' – the naive depiction of common positive opinion – represents a person proud of his or her homeland. The conversation is made sufficiently anonymous that Joy could represent any citizen, anywhere, who is unreflectively proud of his city. The role of Reason is to temper Joy's superficial musings by pointing out that the focus on traditional attributes of praise can allow one to neglect what is important in a deeper sense. If you are born in a place that has been showered with glory, it is all the more difficult for you to achieve notable distinction. If your home city is considered noble, that consideration is owed customarily to the city's wealth, its geography and, in the eyes of the multitude, its livestock and produce. It is worth noting that Reason turns from the impersonal description of what ennobles a city to the accusatory second person ('you say that a land is good . . .'), a technique that would spur a reader to personalize the message of the dialogue: every time you focus unreflectively on a traditionally understood attribute of this or that phenomenon, you might be missing something beneath the surface.

In the second book of the *Remedies*, the focus turns from good to bad fortune. One dialogue presents thoughts about something that was never far from people's minds in Petrarch's day: plague. Reason is ever present as an interlocutor, but this time Reason's counterpart is *Metus*, a Latin word that means 'Fear' but that also has overtones of deep psychological dread:

> Fear: 'I shudder at the plague, which rages far and wide.'[13]
>
> Reason: 'And this, too, is nothing other than a fear of death. Once that is put aside, then a complete sense of tranquillity arises. That said, for those of a great-souled nature, that fear should not only not need to be put aside. It should also, certainly, not be permitted an audience. For is there anything less deserving of a man than to fear ordinary things?'

Just as we have seen in the more private case of his *Secret*, here, in the more public *Remedies*, a theme emerges that, though drawn from a particular occurrence (here the understandable fear of plague), has general relevance: meditation on death.

A bit later the interlocutors proceed:

> Fear: 'I shudder at the plague.'
>
> Reason: 'If a kind of charity towards the human race draws you to this position, then that is something I praise. For there is nothing greater for man than to

take pity on human misfortunes. But if this has to do with you yourself, then that is something with which I take issue. For why should the plague be seen as harmful to any mortal, since it only causes you to do what you will do in any case?'

If in his *Secret*, Petrarch was given to longer, more extended and more circular meanderings, here the points are made in a simpler and more lapidary way: Christian Stoicism for the masses. You are going to die in any case, and the time and place are, for the most part, not up to you. So agonizing, first, about your own mortality and, second, about the manner of its occurrence (by the plague, say) represents nothing so much as selfishness.

The rest of the short dialogues that make up the *Remedies* are quite similar. They are directed towards the ordinary concerns, both positive and negative, of everyday people. They spoke to Petrarch's immediate era more strongly than they did to succeeding generations. For us they help chart Petrarch's evolution as he passed into his old age: concerned most of all with lived ethics, on guard against arrogance in others (to the point of being preachy) and always able to manifest those concerns most pithily in Latin. Another product of Petrarch's mature years shares some of these qualities, though it has more appeal today, written as it was in a kind of white heat.

The *Invective on His Own Ignorance and That of Many Others*, written in 1367 and thus late in life, represents a summing up of Petrarch's complicated personality, even as it distils his own particular conception of what education, learning and even friendship represent. Petrarch had moved from Milan to

Venice in 1361 (to avoid another outbreak of plague), where he remained until 1367. Upon settling in, he had befriended four younger men, each a member of the Venetian aristocracy. We learn from the dedicatory letter to *On His Own Ignorance* that Petrarch was used to gathering with these friends to talk amiably – or so he thought – about literature, philosophy and life. At one of these conversations, however, something happened that caused these younger men to turn against him, offending him deeply and stimulating him to write.

It is worth stopping for a moment to discuss the text both in its physical form and in its genre. *On His Own Ignorance* is one of those precious literary remains from the later Middle Ages and Renaissance that exists in autograph, meaning that we have the very text that Petrarch wrote and annotated in his own hand. There are in fact two versions, one now in Berlin, the other in the Vatican Library.[14] Together, they show the immense work Petrarch put into the text before sending it along to his dedicatee in 1371. The Vatican version, in fact, incorporates marginal annotations Petrarch himself had made in the earlier version. Petrarch tells his dedicatee that he wrote it while travelling on a ship, and from the crabbed marginal annotations, it is not difficult to believe him. He wrote, revised and wrote again, and the pages in the Berlin version tell the story (illus. 22). We see the energy that bubbled up in him when his friendly conversation went awry. And the particular reasons why that conversation soured were meaningful to him precisely because they ran counter to his conception of culture.

As to genre, *On His Own Ignorance* is an invective. Yet here too, subtleties emerge. We possess three other invectives that

22 The earlier (Berlin) version of Petrarch's *De sui ipsius et multorum ignorantia* (Invective on His Own Ignorance and that of Many Others), with marginal annotations in his own hand.

Petrarch penned, and those three, unlike *On His Own Ignorance*, follow the rules of the invective genre. Invective forms part of the rhetoric of praise and blame, or what scholars who study rhetoric call epideictic rhetoric. The rules of that genre imply, in general, a kind of emotional completeness, which is to say that when you are praising someone, you really praise him and when you are heaping reprobation on someone – as in an invective – you pull out all the stops. Petrarch's other invectives can be quite shocking today, occasionally replete with vulgarities as they are.

To take one example, he had encountered an arrogant doctor who had implied that Petrarch, mere poet though he was, should not be taken seriously. More than this, the doctor had said that the long study he himself had put into his discipline meant that he was a philosopher, unlike the lowly poet Petrarch. This condescension rankled Petrarch, and in his *Invective Against a Doctor*, he says, on the one hand, things we would expect from him – for example, that the doctor is no philosopher, that the real search for wisdom (meaning authentic philosophy) consists in self-knowledge and virtuous deeds rather than technical mastery of any given subject, and so on. On the other hand, Petrarch also says things like, 'When I see you despise transitory things, cultivate virtue, pursue true praise, ignore money, aspire to heavenly goals and abandon rich men's latrines – then I shall believe whatever you wish.'[15] Note the mention of latrines. Elsewhere Petrarch denigrates the doctor by saying that his profession compels him to have his hands covered in faeces (using a saltier word). Proud of his profession as a writer, Petrarch goes so far as to say to the doctor that, 'while your hands are examining discharges, mine are writing something' that will be pleasing to future generations.[16] In other words, Petrarch directs his fury at the doctor specifically, goes all out in promoting his own superiority and that of all he does and takes every opportunity, low and high, to criticize the doctor.

It is against this background that we can see why the tenor of *On His Own Ignorance* is so remarkable. For here, instead of the vitriol we see in the other invectives, Petrarch offers a tone that is by turns wistful, exaggeratedly (and somewhat falsely) humble, elegiac and angry. The dedicatory letter, which Petrarch included in his collection of *Letters of Old Age*, sets the stage.[17] Petrarch wrote it to a somewhat younger friend, Donato Albanzani, someone whom he trusted to understand his message. (His trust was not misplaced: Albanzani became one of those key figures who helped in both the literal and the cultural translation of Petrarch's ideas to a larger sphere, translating as he did Petrarch's *On Illustrious Men* into the vernacular.) Petrarch sets the tone for Albanzani – and for any reader – when he suggests about *On His Own Ignorance* that 'you will read it just as you often listen to my fireside chats on winter nights, when I ramble as the impulse moves me. I have called this work a book, but it is really a talk.'[18]

There are two key words in this description, a guide, really, for how Petrarch wants his work to be received: 'ramble' and 'talk'. The word translated as 'ramble' is the Latin verb *fabulo*, which, as one can intuit, has to do with storytelling. Throughout the Italian Renaissance, after Petrarch, many Italian thinkers would believe, as did Petrarch, that the real pursuit of wisdom – philosophy in its authentic rather than in its institutionally located sense – had precisely to do with story-telling.

One such thinker, Angelo Poliziano (1454–1494), would enunciate this predilection quite literally when he wrote that 'stories' – *fabellae* in Poliziano's Latin – 'are not only the first beginnings of philosophy. Stories are also – and just as often – philosophy's instrument.'[19]

Stories, conversation or (to return to the second important word in Petrarch's prefatory letter) 'talk', or *colloquium* in Latin: a crucial Italian Renaissance tendency that Petrarch inaugurated forcefully was that of linking eloquent conversation with wisdom.[20] *Colloquium* means more than just 'talk', especially the way Petrarch is using the word here. It implies that there will be a listener on the other end, that the listener in question will also, if he desires, have responses to offer, and that this reciprocal process will lead to a conversation in which meaningful participation produces shared wisdom. As we shall see it is precisely the tendency to seek wisdom in other, more rigid ways to which Petrarch most strongly objects in his *On His Own Ignorance*.

On His Own Ignorance is indeed a rambling work. Petrarch takes quite a while to reveal the specific event that precipitated his need to write it. It is worth following Petrarch's train of thought for a bit, since in his vehement defence of his own approach and denigration of that of his opponents, he provides a manifesto of an influential strain of Italian Renaissance thought that lasted for decades, if not centuries, after him. Early on, he reveals that a problem has emerged with these erstwhile friends, one that he believes has to do with envy. And yet, he asks, what can they envy? He answers, 'They can't envy my knowledge or my eloquence. They assert that I have not a trace of knowledge. As for eloquence, if I have any at all, they despise it as our modern philosophers do, and reject it as unworthy of learned men.'[21] This statement represents the crux of the matter: Petrarch has come to believe that real wisdom must be coupled with eloquence in expression to be effective, a theme on which he will expatiate throughout *On His Own Ignorance*. He soon reveals what it is precisely that they envy: 'my reputation, small as it is, and the fame I have won in this life'.[22]

'Small as it is': this sort of 'humility' wends its way throughout *On His Own Ignorance*. As to the notional envy, Petrarch's description thereof tells us where he really wants to go, which is to highlight, to condemn and (to be frank) to parody the sort of learning prized by his friends.

One of them, Petrarch admits, is indeed quite learned. And yet, 'Learning is an instrument of madness for many, and of pride for nearly everyone.'[23] What sorts of things does this gentleman know? 'This fourth fellow knows about wild beasts, birds, and fish. He knows how many hairs a lion has in its mane, how many feathers a hawk has in its tail, and how many coils an octopus wraps around a castaway.' This type of thing goes on for a bit, until Petrarch ends his litany of animal facts by saying that this friend 'knows that moles are blind, that bees are deaf, and that the crocodile is the only animal that moves its upper jaw'.[24] There then follows one of the piece's most interesting passages, one that because of its unique blend of contradictions deserves to be quoted in full:

> In most cases, these things are false, as was revealed when many such animals were brought to our part of the world. Clearly, the facts were not known to those

reporting them, and they were more readily believed or more freely invented because the animals were not present. Yet even if they were true, they would contribute absolutely nothing to the happiness of our life. What use is it, I ask, to know the nature of beasts and birds and fish and snakes, and to ignore or neglect our human nature, the purpose of our birth, or whence we come and whither we are bound?[25]

This passage emerges as one of the most important ones in all of *On His Own Ignorance*.

It should be said that, with his listing all in a row of a series of recondite animal facts, Petrarch is drawing for the most part on the ancient Roman naturalist writer Pliny the Elder, whose *Natural History* served as a repository of knowledge about the natural world. And Petrarch is of course parodying a bloviating academic, so puffed up on his own field-specific knowledge that he loses the forest for the trees. So in a sense the passage has a clear message: too much hyper-specialization, at the expense of a larger vision of what human wisdom can represent, is a bad thing. Yet, looked at more broadly, this passage also represents one of the most central and controversial elements of the humanities-oriented turn that many Italian intellectuals took decisively after Petrarch.

On the one hand, there is an embryonic defence of empiricism. Petrarch's critique of his unnamed friend has mostly to do with verification, or a lack thereof. Parading facts about animals that are drawn only from texts can seem foolish, especially so when the animals in question are brought forwards, examined and proven not to match the accounts given in texts. To be clear, when Petrarch says 'the facts were not known to those reporting them' (the word for 'not known' in Latin is *incomperta*), he is saying that and that alone. He is not, in other words, offering a theory of empiricism, such as later thinkers like Francis Bacon (1561–1626) would sketch out, as they focused on the gathering of evidence, the need for replicable experiments, and so on. His critique of assertion without evidence is used here primarily as a rhetorical element, a way of pushing back against one of the people who criticized him. But if we should not overestimate what Petrarch is saying here, it would be imprudent as well to underestimate it. For his critique at least presents the seeds of an appreciation for evidence that would emerge later as one of the cornerstones of modern science.

This makes it all the more noteworthy that Petrarch turns away from this proto-empirical utterance and moves instead to a full-throated disparagement of the whole enterprise of natural science as it stood in his own day. When he asks why it is relevant at all to know natural scientific facts, if one has not first focused on the purpose of human life, he foreshadows the principal concern of Italian Renaissance intellectual life for the next five generations of thinkers to come. It is, in the end, a quite striking juxtaposition: a nascent empiricism versus a critique thereof. This seeming turn from natural science represents one of the reasons Italian Renaissance intellectual life has been at times subject to critique.

One of the great historians of modern science, George Sarton, disapproved of this tendency in just these terms. About the intellectual movement which Petrarch shaped so authoritatively, Sarton wrote that 'from the philosophical as

well as from the scientific standpoint this was undoubtedly
a regression . . . The only remedy which could have cured
them was a direct appeal to nature – experimental science
– but this they hardly understood.'[26] There were many others
who shared this notion, and it is an opinion of which echoes
can be heard even today: that Petrarch and those Italian intellectuals who followed in his wake represented agents of
cultural retardation, rather than advancement, and that by
looking backwards to antiquity, they arrested the progress of
(scientific) modernity.

Yet Sarton and others like him missed something important about what Petrarch and other Italian Renaissance intellectuals were up to. To understand this factor, a deeper dive
into Petrarch's *On His Own Ignorance* and its context is needed.
Petrarch reports that what got his friends' ire up was a seeming mis-statement regarding Aristotle: 'At first they were
amazed, and then angered, for they felt that my words ran
counter to their sect and its ancestral laws.'[27] 'Sect' and 'ancestral laws': these are the two most meaningful expressions
in the entire work. The word that Petrarch uses for 'sect' in
Latin is *haeresis*, a word that is a direct Latin borrowing from
the Greek, whose origins lie in the Greek verb *haereô*, which
at its root means 'separating', 'choosing' and 'cutting apart'.
A *haeresis* originally meant a choice, in a fairly neutral way.
Over time, the word came to signify a choice one made to
join a group, and sometimes even the wrong choice of a religious group, as the word 'heresy' implies. So when Petrarch
says his friends' anger emerged only after they realized he
would not be part of their 'sect', all of those resonances are
there in that one word. Religious overtones, the implication

that members of a sect close themselves off from salutary outside contact and an implicit declaration of one's own freedom from those seeming strictures: all combine in Petrarch's formulation. Who are the members of the sect in question? Aristotelians. We will have more to say about this aspect in a moment, but the other expression deserves comment first: 'ancestral laws'.

In this case the Latin words are *paternae leges*, which might just as well be translated as 'the laws of your fathers'. But what laws? And who are the fathers? Answering these questions allows us to decode Petrarch's anger, even as doing so unlocks what is most important about Petrarch's protest here and the cultural movement he helped to foster. For what is really at stake is institutional culture and the side-effects it can produce.

By Petrarch's maturity, universities in Europe were over two centuries old. The University of Bologna, for example, where Petrarch studied law, was in operation from the eleventh century and became the leading centre for the study of Roman law (and thus the birthplace of the study of the modern civil law tradition). The University of Paris received a charter (an official document of recognition) from the French king in 1200 and was then formally recognized by Pope Innocent III in 1215. Paris quickly became Europe's leading centre for the study of theology. In both of those cases, as in those of other universities, the formalities (naming, chartering and so on) followed, chronologically, the basic practices themselves. In other words, universities by Petrarch's day represented a key part of culture and a taken-for-granted fact: higher education was there to stay.[28]

Looking at the history of universities up to that point, their evolution is striking. They began as places of excitement. A 'master' (meaning a teacher, *magister* in Latin) might have fascinating new ideas on some topic, say in law or philosophy. Those ideas would prove so interesting that groups of eager students would gather around him, to learn from him. Gradually more students would gather and organize into groups, and that master as well as others like him would aggregate in a certain part of the city. This early aggregation is why certain parts of European cities tend strongly to be marked by the medieval presence of their university (like the Left Bank in Paris, for instance). In places like that, gradually, buildings were endowed and erected, rituals developed and patterns established that lasted for centuries. There is a reason why we still wear clerical robes at university graduation ceremonies and why we still have degree titles invented in the Western Middle Ages. BA, 'Bachelor of Arts', was originally the *baccalaureus artium* degree, which would qualify one for entry into coursework that would lead to a *magister artium*, or 'Master of Arts' degree, which afforded one the recognized ability to teach (*licentia docendi* in Latin). After studying the liberal arts in an intensive fashion, you would then be qualified, if the long, rigorous curriculum did not prove too daunting, to enter study in one of the three professional schools – law, medicine and theology – where you could earn a 'doctoral' degree.

These traditions, some of which still exist today, should not mask the fact that universities were, in a sense, 'accidental', at least in their early phases. They arose where they did because that was where the excitement was, at least originally.

To stick with law and philosophy, in both cases rediscovery spurred much of this excitement. As to law, the big event was the eleventh-century rediscovery of the *Corpus iuris civilis*, the 'Body of Civil Law', which represents a collection, gathered after the Roman Empire had fallen, of key documents in ancient Roman law. It was when the *Corpus* was still 'new' that things were most exciting, when students began to flock to Bologna to hear lectures on the text, and when the University established itself as the leading place to think about law in Europe. The study of civil law based on the *Corpus* grew side by side with the study of religious (or Canon) law and, before long, Bologna was the place to be for both. Similarly, when it came to philosophy, the rediscovery of Aristotle's works was the key event that propelled change. Most of Aristotle's works had been lost to the West in the Middle Ages, as knowledge of Greek declined and interests shifted elsewhere (some of his works on logic had been translated into Latin and were known in the Middle Ages). But Byzantine intellectuals continued to study Aristotle, as did Islamic thinkers, a development that assisted in the remarkable rise of medieval Islamic science and philosophy. Islam arrived in Spain in the eighth century and took hold there for centuries; and there were some Greek speakers in southern Italy throughout the Middle Ages.

When in the eleventh and twelfth centuries a newly buoyant economy led to more resources for and interest in learning and culture, a series of Latin translations of Aristotle's works emerged. Some were done directly from the Greek sources, whereas others were from Arabic intermediaries. Either way, the presence of Aristotle in the West coincided with the take-off of universities. And soon, at a number of universities, much of the arts curriculum and a good part of theology as well (for which philosophy was thought of as an ancillary discipline) became heavily inflected by Aristotelian texts and problems. This dominance was so strong that medieval, university-based thinkers called Aristotle, simply, 'the philosopher', without needing to name him. It was precisely to this outsized place of one thinker that Petrarch was objecting. As he, finally, arrives at the specific incident that precipitated conflict with his friends, he reveals precisely what he means.

Petrarch recounts how meetings with his friends would normally unfold: 'They used to propose some Aristotelian problem or some such thing about animals for discussion. I would remain silent, or joke, or introduce some other topic.'[29] So far, so good. This type of interaction was something relatively normal for literate medieval and Renaissance people to do: gather together, discuss some intellectual topic and let the conversation play itself out. However, these conversations, we infer, began to be coloured with a particular hue. After his friends would set out the problem they wanted to discuss, Petrarch would often react, he says, in this way: 'Sometimes I would smile and ask how Aristotle could have known things for which there is no inherent rational basis and for which direct experience is impossible.'[30] Again, these comments are tantalizing, because they seem to get us so close to modern theories of scientific explanation. For 'no inherent rational basis', Petrarch says in Latin *cuius nulla ratio esset*, which we can render most literally as 'for which there is no reason'. The key word here, 'reason', or *ratio* in Latin, can mean various things: 'reason', 'argument', 'reckoning', 'rational explanation', 'calculation', 'account' and 'plan', among other things. And of course

Petrarch means all of those things and none of them. What he is really getting at is that, whatever Aristotelian or other problem his friends may be posing, it cannot thoroughly be explained using mental reasoning alone.

When Petrarch says his friends are discussing things as facts 'for which direct experience is impossible', the Latin word Petrarch uses (for 'direct experience') is *experimentum*. Again it is an enticing word, one which makes us think first of 'experiment' and 'experimentation' and that has a range of meanings that include 'proof' and 'observation' as well as 'direct experience' (the translation chosen here). Like so much else in medieval and Renaissance culture, you can choose to read more or less into these sorts of phrases. In this case, Petrarch evokes the sort of language that, much later, became part of the lexicon of modern science. But this and other such evocations should be seen as seeds, seeds that became part of intellectual life, floated over different chronological terrains and only much later took root and grew to fruition.

In any case, Petrarch's concern here is much more imme-diate, intentional and purposeful, as we can see when he moves on in his account, relating his friends' reactions after he would, occasionally, question something having to do with Aristotle:

> They would be amazed and silently angered, and would look at me as a blasphemer for requiring more than that man's authority as proof of fact. It was clear that, from philosophers and eager lovers of wisdom, we had become Aristotelians – or rather, Pythagoreans, having revived that laughable custom, whereby they

were allowed to ask after nothing, unless 'he' said it.
And as Cicero relates, 'he' was Pythagoras.[31]

First, a bit of background: in the many legends that had
accrued in antiquity regarding Pythagoras, one was that his
followers (even centuries later) were so enthralled by him
and his reputation for wisdom that, to confirm the veracity
of any proposition, statement, or position, it was enough for
them to say 'he said so', or *ipse dixit*, in Latin (as Cicero had
indeed related the tale).[32] For Cicero, this tendency, dogmatic
as it seemed, had betokened a kind of ideological rigidity: a
stifling of curiosity and the spirit of real philosophy. Petrarch
employs this notion in the same spirit.

As always, too, the words Petrarch chooses to use are significant, most especially when he writes that 'from philosophers
and eager lovers of wisdom, we had become Aristotelians'.
Petrarch uses the key words – 'philosophers' and 'lovers of
wisdom' – in what grammarians would call 'apposition': they
are separated by the word 'and', but in truth the word 'and'
is used as a connector. What Petrarch is saying is that 'philosophy' and the 'love of wisdom' are the same. This notion
too had been part of the legends pertaining to Pythagoras,
who, when asked by a ruler whether he was 'wise' (*sophos*) in
Greek, said that he was not wise but that he was a 'lover of
wisdom' (a *philosophos*).[33]

We see Petrarch clarify his position regarding Aristotle:
'Now, I believe that Aristotle was a great man and a polymath.
But he was still human and could therefore have been ignor-
ant of some things, or even of many things.'[34] We can understand what Petrarch is up to here by stepping back in time a

bit, to Dante, who had provided a sketch in the fourth canto of the *Inferno* of 'virtuous pagans', which is to say pre- or non-Christian people who had nonetheless lived lives of virtue in various respects. They were not permitted to enter purgatory or heaven, never having known Christ. Yet they were spared eternal damnation, because of their virtue, and lived in a kind of limbo. In that part of the *Inferno* Dante referred to Aristotle as the *maestro di color che sanno* – the 'master of those who know'. Dante had further said that all the other members of the *filosofica famiglia* – the 'philosophical family', meaning philosophers broadly conceived – 'looked up him' (to Aristotle, that is) 'and paid honour to him' – even Plato, Aristotle's teacher.[35] The language implies a reverence so strong that, when all was said and done, after time had erased the vagaries of earthly tradition, all philosophers, from all times, simply stood in awe of Aristotle and his superhuman greatness. For Dante, in other words, Aristotle's pre-eminence among all philosophers was an assumed fact. It was something he had fully absorbed in his studies of medieval philosophical and theological learning, even as he went on to present, in his *Divine Comedy*, a creative and beguiling synthesis of that tradition that has stood the test of time.

The assumption about Aristotle's pre-eminence was so strong because it was so often unarticulated. It is precisely this tendency against which Petrarch pushes back in *On His Own Ignorance*. Aristotle was great, yes. He was a 'polymath' who, because of the range of what his work covered, is even now worthy of great admiration. But he was not the only philosopher, and remember (Petrarch is saying): Aristotle was a human being. He could err just like the rest of us, and our responsibility as intellectuals is to remember that fact and to temper our reverence for Aristotle with the spirit of free enquiry.

That, at least, is one way of reading Petrarch and what he is up to in *On His Own Ignorance*. Another way emerges from a later passage in the text, when he openly asserts precisely what it was to which his erstwhile friends objected, especially when it came to ethics and to what makes a person happy: 'that I do not worship Aristotle', or, in Latin, *quod Aristotelem non adoro*.[36] That last word, *adoro*, can indeed mean worship, as translated here. It also carries the meaning one might infer in English: 'adore' or 'cherish'. If we were to read it as the latter meaning, then the interpretation offered above (that Petrarch is objecting to narrow-minded intellectual dogmatism) would seem not just the right, but the only possible interpretation of his meaning here.

However, immediately following that pronouncement Petrarch offers a statement that, in effect, complicates his meaning and how to read him here. For the moment after he relates his friends' critique (that he does not 'worship' Aristotle), he says this: 'But I have someone else whom I worship.' And of course, the person to whom he refers is none other than Jesus Christ, who 'does not promise empty and frivolous conjectures, about fallacious things, which serve no purpose and rest on no solid basis'.[37] As we have seen in Petrarch's angry letter to Boccaccio, one of his fears was that university-based philosopher-theologians were diving so deep into Aristotle that they were removing themselves from true Christianity. So, on the surface, Petrarch's message is clear: culture needs a reorientation, buttressed by good authentic classical Latin, but focused on Christianity.

Yet beneath the surface, there is another, more powerful and lasting meaning, one that represents everything that Sarton and his ilk missed (and that some still miss) about Petrarch and what was best about the Italian intellectual tradition he inaugurated. Petrarch's real objection is not against Aristotle but rather against Aristotelians. This is to say that he is objecting to uncritical adherents of Aristotle. Aristotle here is as much a symbol as a historical reality. As to historical reality, it is true that, as we have seen, there were certain facets of Aristotle's thought difficult to reconcile with medieval Christian orthodoxy. The two most prominent instances were Aristotle's ambiguous positions on the question whether the human soul was mortal or immortal and his belief that the cosmos was eternal, rather than something that had been created by God (as Genesis suggested and as was Christian orthodoxy). Still, Petrarch is willing to listen to, indeed to study, Aristotle, but with one crucial shift in perspective: Aristotle was one voice in what Petrarch began to see as a polyphony of ancient voices that all deserved study but which needed to be reconciled to the reality in which he found himself. For Petrarch, that reality was Christian as he understood it, and no amount of verbal contortions could make Aristotle say something he had not said on the soul, say, or on the eternity of the cosmos.

As much as Aristotle represents a reality, both as a historical figure and as a set of philosophical texts, his symbolic valence is as important, if not more so, in understanding Petrarch's real achievement. Symbolically, Aristotle stands for a curriculum and, more, for institutions and the way they can, consciously or not, replicate themselves in an uncritical way. Petrarch forcefully took the deliberate position of an outsider to existing institutions.

That was his most important achievement: to have the courage to chart his own course and to recognize that there are times when individuals need to break from the traditions they have inherited. This achievement is not without its layers of irony. Petrarch had trained at universities, and the many Italian Renaissance intellectuals after him who consciously adopted this outsider pose did so as well.[38] There were even those from within the late medieval university community who objected to the rigidity of genre that university-sanctioned forms of writing permitted. Jean Gerson (1363–1429), for example, who was chancellor of the University of Paris, revived a genre of writing that he thought could contribute more to problems outside the university world than standard forms of university writing could then do.[39] So Petrarch's outsider stance should not be overestimated in its originality, scope and importance. But it should not be underestimated, either. It was a bequest he gave, not only to the Italian Renaissance, but to northern luminaries like Erasmus and, late in the sixteenth century, Michel de Montaigne (1533–1592), who with his introspective brilliance said: 'I never saw a monster or marvel greater than myself.'[40]

This was Petrarch's other meaningful contribution, something that emerges far more powerfully in his Latin prose than in his poetry, whether vernacular or Latin: by putting himself and his contemporaries under intense examination, he allows us to see ourselves as real human beings, flawed and subject to emotion. It is paradoxical. For Petrarch, Latin prose, though a secondary language learned in schools, was the language far more suited to honest self-expression. We see self-doubt, anger, sadness, pride, vanity and other emotions. These are present, of course, in his poetry, but, bound by rules of meter as his poetry was, it was by design more inclined to construction, to artifice and to levels of polish that make the emotional message something for which one needs to dig. In works such as his letters and invectives, the emotions are all on the surface.

This resonance holds for *On His Own Ignorance*. When all is said and done Petrarch finally reveals what it was precisely that led to the final break with his former friends: he said something un-Aristotelian about virtue. In his *Nicomachean Ethics*, Aristotle had developed lasting positions on human virtue, or excellence. In one sense virtues could be seen as means between extremes. Bravery, for instance, can be viewed as a mean between cowardice and foolhardiness. Virtues could also be seen as capacities which everyone possesses but which need to be practised to develop in full. You become brave only by repeatedly performing brave acts, you become a charitable person only by performing acts of charity, and so on.[41] Aristotle's *Nicomachean Ethics* was one of those many Aristotelian works that were translated into Latin and that became the subject of intense study and commentary in universities, with highly technical positions having been developed regarding the virtues and many other subjects related to ethics that Aristotle had raised.

Petrarch does not tell us what it was specifically that he said, but whatever it was, it must have been an error, or something that did not accord with stock Aristotelian positions. We can infer the environment from Petrarch's tone: an older,

respected man in the company of brash younger men up on
the latest new developments in their field, preening and
boasting of their own knowledge, even as they were also test-
ing the older man, seeing what he knew, wondering where
the gaps in his knowledge lay, wondering where they might
be able to make their own mark. And then we see the older
man, having seen much in his life: intimates who have died,
rulers whom death has felled, academic fads that have come
and gone. The incident, whatever it was, occurred and the
actual break – which had been simmering, perhaps – finally
came to full fruition.

But what was it, really, that Petrarch saw as lacking, or
flawed, in his friends' conduct? On one hand, it was precisely
what he said about their tendency (in his view, of course)
towards groupthink – from 'philosophers we have become
Aristotelians'. On the other hand, there was something else,
something that had to do with Aristotle's texts themselves,
which we can observe as Petrarch moves on in his invective
and asserts, regarding Aristotle: 'I admit I take no pleasure
in his style.'[42] Is that all there is? Form rather than content?
No. For Petrarch there was more. Petrarch relates his history
with Aristotle. He goes on to say that he has 'read' and 'heard'
Aristotle (the latter signifying that he had attended university
lectures on Aristotle). 'And as to what I have learned,' Petrarch
goes on, 'I do know somewhat more than what I knew before.'
Fair enough. 'But still: my spirit was what it had been before.
My will was the same. I was the same.'[43] What use is more
learning, especially in a field like ethics (the subject-matter
around which the incident between Petrarch and his friends
turned), if you are not somehow changed by what you have

learned? If you do not become a better person? In the end, Petrarch asserts, 'it is a better thing to will the good, than to know the truth.'[44]

For Petrarch, real moral philosophers, meaning those who write about and teach ethics in the most respectable way, are those whose intention it is to make their readers and students good. Later Petrarch will re-emphasize that he has nothing whatsoever against Aristotle, only against the seeming sectarianism that can develop among professed Aristotelians.[45] Petrarch stresses that there were a number of fine philosophers who existed before Aristotle, so that yet again the reader infers that history is needed in any matter of intellectual moment.

To understand Aristotle, Petrarch's assumption goes, you need to understand him in context, to realize that, though he was a great philosopher, he was also just one philosopher among a number. One of that number was Aristotle's predecessor and teacher, Plato. Augustine had said that Plato was 'closest to us', meaning that of all the pagan philosophers, Plato had come the closest to anticipating certain parts of Christianity, especially when it came to the immortality of the human soul and merit-based rewards and punishments after death.[46]

Petrarch was well aware of the opinion of his great hero Augustine in this regard. That is one among many reasons why Petrarch wrote one of the most celebrated, if sometimes misunderstood, lines in *On His Own Ignorance*: 'Plato is praised by the better men, Aristotle by the greater number' (*a maioribus Plato, Aristoteles laudatur a pluribus*).[47] Petrarch is not so much voicing a preference here for Platonic over against Aristotelian philosophy. The truth is that he did not know enough to do so in a detailed way. Petrarch boasts about having Plato's works in his own library (at least sixteen of them, he says, though elsewhere he would admit he cannot read them, because they are in Greek, a language he never mastered). Rather, he is making the case (as he had done in the story of why he 'abandoned' his vernacular poetry) that crowds cannot be trusted, and that if one thinker or school of thought represents the majority of what preoccupies a crowd of people, then some rethinking is needed. Petrarch sometimes pursued this train of thought to such an extent that it became misanthropic. And it is certainly the case that his own ego often got in the way of his appreciation of life, rendering him at times depressed, angry and overly voluble about his own superiority. Yet those psychological tendencies are personal matters.

Soon after his statement on Plato and Aristotle, Petrarch brings *On His Own Ignorance* to a conclusion, his passion having cooled a little. This whole episode had happened while he was residing in the city of Venice, close to Padua, where the Carrara family, his then patrons, were based. About Venice, he writes that it is a city possessed of a great amount of freedom, including an 'excessive freedom of speech' (*verborum longe nimia est libertas*), reflecting how he had been stung by his friends' unexpected attack.[48] Petrarch in fact had been so impressed by Venice and its institutions that he had planned on leaving his own private library to the city, in the hope that his collection of books might be used as the foundation of a library beneficial to the general scholarly public.[49] But it was not to be. Petrarch retired to his country home in Arquà, outside Padua, removing himself from city life.

When it comes to *On His Own Ignorance*, more important is what he left behind: a kind of anti-dogmatism that can be, and has been, interpreted in many ways. In the text itself, it is clear that one of Petrarch's key concerns is religion, at least on the surface. His young philosopher-friends are so puffed up with pride, so focused on their Aristotelian texts, that they have forgotten Christian humility. Yet some scholars have interpreted Petrarch as an early avatar of a kind of secularism.[50] The reason lies in his anti-institutionalism. In the case of *On His Own Ignorance*, the institutions against which he positions himself are universities, even if he does not say it in so many words. The kinds of positions he satirizes (excessive attention to meaningless scholarly details on his friends' part, and so on) had their roots in universities and in the tendency of intellectuals, when gathered together over time, to do two things: to hyper-specialize, with every generation digging deeper and deeper, even if the field of endeavour narrows overall; and to engage in a kind of groupthink, whereby certain unarticulated assumptions become standard. In this case, the guiding assumption was that Aristotle was 'the' instead of 'a' philosopher. But versions of these 'sectarian' tendencies (to recall Petrarch's use of the word 'sect') appear in many institutions; and negative reactions to them are present in every accusation of 'political correctness', whether justified or not. An early version of secularism, in this case, means advocating a sense of separation from group norms.

Needless to say, in our day the word 'secularism' strongly implies much more than this, recalling atheism, anti-religiosity and a sense that humanly created political norms represent the best, and real, roots of civil life. Petrarch is far from all of

ELTEMPO CHE
RINOVA E MIE
SOSPIRI PER
LADOLCE M
EMORIA D
IQVEL GIO
RNO CHE
FV PRINCI
PIO AD SI L
VNGHI MARTIRI

this. True, he criticizes the Church, or more specifically the papal court in Avignon, as a den of vice, with those who should be promoting evangelical poverty more devoted to the pleasures of the flesh. In one respect this line of criticism represents the view of a relative insider, the opinions of a person who has seen an institution up close and who thus can see the underbelly hidden from outside view. For Petrarch, too, his criticism of the papacy's residency in Avignon was tightly bound to his almost mystical view of Rome – as a place that once served as the home of the greatest empire the world had ever known and that could rise up again, if only the right leaders would take control, buttressed by the right religion.

If only. Petrarch first drafted *On His Own Ignorance* in a white heat in 1367. For the next few years, amid other cares, he revised it, finishing the version we have now in 1371. By that time, he had left Venice behind. In his life he had fathered two children. One of them, Giovanni, had died of an outbreak

23 Detail of a miniature by Francesco di Antonio del Chierico in a 1476 parchment copy of Petrarch's *Triunfi* that depicts Petrarch resting his head on a rock.

of plague in 1361, something that Petrarch noted in his beloved Virgil manuscript. Another, his daughter, Francesca, married, had children and stayed close to her father, moving to Arquà together with him.

This last period of Petrarch's life was marked by a sense of retreat from the world. He stayed in the sleepy town of Arquà, engaged in contemplation, and continued as ever to revise his works. One of these was his *Triumphs*, a work of vernacular poetry whose final part represents the 'if only' side of Petrarch's consciousness better than any other (illus. 23). He had begun it back in 1351, when he had decided in his heart to move to Italy.[51] There is one side of the *Triumphs* that relates intimately to Italy and to one of Petrarch's biggest influences, Dante, however much Petrarch tried overtly to downplay the presence of the poet in his mind.

The structure of the *Triumphs* tells the story. A 'triumph' in the ancient Roman world signified a public ceremony held to honour a victorious military leader upon his return from battle. Crowned with laurel, clad in a purple toga, the leader would head a public procession that included his soldiers and the spoils of war they had won. As we have seen, Petrarch was enamoured of public, ritualized ceremony, having arranged for himself, on the Capitoline Hill in Rome, a ceremony in which he was feted as a poet and given a laurel crown. So on the one hand, Petrarch brought his own, antiquity-loving sensibility to the *Triumphs*. On the other, he wrote them in *terza rima*, the meter of Dante's *Divine Comedy* – sets of three lines ('tercets') in iambic pentameter with a rhyming system that allowed the tercets to interconnect. The progress and structure of the *Triumphs* also hint at the Dantean spectre that haunted Petrarch. For they tell of a kind of journey for the protagonist (Petrarch), who is accompanied by a guide, from the earthly to the heavenly realm, a structure that in some respects resembled that of Dante's *Divine Comedy*.

If that Dantean background is there, Petrarch nevertheless makes the *Triumphs* his own. There are six *Triumphs*, which follow each other, each superseding the last: the *Triumph of Love* (or Cupid), the *Triumph of Chastity*, the *Triumph of Death*, the *Triumph of Fame*, the *Triumph of Time* and the *Triumph of Eternity*. It is easy enough to see the basic message: Chastity (meaning virtuous modesty and non-sexual love) triumphs over 'love' (meaning desire, something that for Petrarch is symbolized by Cupid and his arrow). Death erases all of those human, worldly affairs, only to have its own place taken by fame, which outlasts death and 'pulls man from his tomb and gives him life'.[52] But time, personified, rushes on, 'faster than a falcon after his prey', to such a point that Petrarch, who has set himself within the poems as an observer, asks: 'What more is this life than one day?'[53] Even fame, in other words, will be superseded by time's ineluctable progress, time which leaves cities in ruins and erases all of the best work of humanity: 'Time, avaricious, conquers and thieves; Fame, so-called, is but a second death; and there is no defence for either fame or death. And it is thus that time triumphs over all of the world's great names!'[54] It is with this sentiment, really, that there is one aspect left, one part of God's empire that goes beyond the phenomena we can see, hear or even imagine: eternity.

For Petrarch – and arguably for us all – this set of problems is not just about literature. They represent, instead, the

key mysteries of human life, however much we live without
having them in the front of our minds: what remains of us
after we die, if anything? After reputations fade, what then?
Will anything persist after, or if, the physical world of recognizable phenomena fades from view? To understand Petrarch's
Triumph of Eternity, we need to see, or at least to glimpse, how
thinkers in his era approached the problem. In this respect,
there is no more important theory to appreciate than that of
the Resurrection, a belief that developed alongside theories
about the nature of the human soul and the nature of the
human person.

Briefly, the idea was that, when physical death occurred,
the human soul survived and was punished or rewarded based
on the person's conduct in life. Importantly, 'person' was
understood as a unity of soul and body, form and matter.
Then there was time, which would at some point end (as the
sequence of Petrarch's own *Triumphs* indicates). When that
culminating moment would occur was not known to human-
kind, since the decision rested with God alone. But when
God did decide (in other words, at the end of time), the souls
of the deceased would be united to bodies once again – and
not to metaphorical bodies but to real, 'physical' bodies. This
belief persisted and in fact is still doctrinally on the books in
the Roman Catholic Church. In a religious sense, it reflects
an important conviction: one of the reasons that Christ was
physically resurrected (after his death by crucifixion) was to
guarantee something like that possibility for human beings.
Paul's first letter to the Corinthians had pointed in this direction: 'But now is Christ risen from the dead, and become the
first-fruits of them that slept. For since by man came death,

by man came also the resurrection of the dead. For as in Adam all die, even so in Christ all shall be made alive.'[55] Christ's resurrection, in short, served as a guarantor for eventual human resurrection.

However, beyond the religious and doctrinal sense there was – and is – a more pertinent and vexing difficulty: is a person a person if his or her soul is separate from his or her body? Today it is easier to assume, following the legacy of the seventeenth-century philosopher Descartes, that we possess an immaterial 'mind', which is real but which is, at its most basic level, unconnected to matter. But this pure immateriality is not what pre-modern thinkers had in mind when they spoke of the 'soul'. For them, and certainly for Petrarch, soul and body were intimately connected in establishing real personhood. The result was that, though it was possible to separate them conceptually, that very separation – such as occurred after death – represented a source of longing, a belief that the person as such could only be a person when soul and body were reunited. So: resurrection.

All of this is what makes Petrarch's *Triumph of Eternity* such a meaningful work and one that serves, fittingly, as a capstone to his life, not least because he wrote it in the last year of his earthly existence. It begins as follows, with a question befitting an old man looking back on his years:

Then when I saw nothing under heaven that was steady and stationary, entirely dismayed I turned to my heart and said: 'In what do you trust?' It replied: 'In the Lord, who unfailingly keeps covenant with whoever has faith in Him. But I see quite well that the world has scorned me. And I grasp indeed what I am, what I was. And I see time go by – no, I see it fly and I'd like to complain but I don't know about whom. For the fault is mine alone, since for too long I should have opened my eyes and not dawdled until the end, though in truth even now do I delay overmuch. And yet: divine graces have never been late, and I do place my hope in them, that, within me, they will have deep and extraordinary effects.' So I spoke, and so my heart replied. If these things are unstable that heaven causes to turn and that it controls, after so many orbits, how will it all end?[56]

How indeed?

Though by now this tendency will be familiar, it is worth noting that we see yet again Petrarch's self-doubt. He 'turns to his heart' to ask in what his heart trusts and, though the reflexive answer is automatic and assumed ('in the Lord'), his heart still has doubts as it considers the world and the way earthly existence, with all its foibles, antagonisms and necessarily unrequited desires, has 'scorned' him. The word translated as 'scorned' is, in Italian, *schernito*, a word that also carries overtones of 'mockery'. It is as if Petrarch (or his heart) is saying that the world (meaning other people) has jeered at him: even now, even as an old man, when he has achieved success – even when, in short, he should know better. But it is characterological, this problem he has of thinking that everyone is always looking at him, judging him, mocking him. His heart seems aware of all this, suggesting that it is long past time that he 'open his eyes', meaning that he forego the attractions of the world (the fame, the competition, the endless disappointments) and embrace contemplation and the Lord. Even now, though, he persists in putting that moment off.

Still, there is hope, since if the Lord prefers to bestow grace upon you, by definition, it cannot be too late, since anything the Lord decides is determined at the right moment. Petrarch (his heart) is saying that he is, perhaps, finally ready to embrace the 'deep and extraordinary effects' that divine grace will have on him. Still, the question remains: 'if these things are unstable that heaven causes to turn and that it controls, after so many orbits, how will it all end?'

Like the theory of the Resurrection, the unarticulated assumptions that underlie Petrarch's last question seem unfamiliar today. Petrarch reflects, embraces, but also questions a widespread belief that everything that can be sensed was in motion and unstable, but that there was also a realm that was stable, in which the planets rotated. It was a set of beliefs that went back to Aristotle and to the Graeco-Egyptian thinker Ptolemy, in which it was believed that there were 'fixed stars', meaning heavenly bodies, such as distant stars, that seemed never to move; and that there were 'crystalline spheres': the orbits in which the planets rotated, thought to be fixed as well ('the things that heaven causes to turn'). Yet if even 'these things are unstable', what does it all mean? Are even the physical heavens unstable, though they appear so perfect in their patterns? 'How', Petrarch asks, 'will it all end?' It is the purpose of the *Triumph of Eternity* to answer this question poetically, an enterprise in which Petrarch shows himself in full, even if, as befits a poet, he does so by means of allusions, veiled statements and metaphor.

As his mind was turning over the question of endings, he says: 'to me there appeared a world that was new, motionless and eternal with respect to age.'[57] This world, that of Eternity, suddenly appeared as something new: familiar and recognizable in a way but also different in its permanence and beauty. Petrarch echoes the Book of Revelation: 'And I saw a new heaven and a new earth: for the first heaven and the first earth were passed away, and there was no more sea.'[58] So Petrarch's language would have rung familiar bells for readers. But as Petrarch moves on, he finds a way of integrating philosophical ideas about unity and time with his poetic endeavour:

> What a wonder I experienced when I saw standing still, in one point, that which never does stand still, but rather in its discursive motion is accustomed to change all things. Its three parts did I see, drawn together into one alone, with that one being still in such a way that it hurried not, as it was wont to do.[59]

Opaque as it might seem, Petrarch is talking about time.

The 'three parts' are past, present and future, which he sees 'drawn into one alone', meaning the present. The present, in normal circumstances, never stands still. One experiences the present as if it is in motion, since it soon becomes the past, even as it verges inevitably towards the future. But Petrarch sees it become 'still' (the word he uses is *ferma*, which means the opposite of 'in motion') (illus. 24, 25). Petrarch points to time in the way God was believed to experience it: past, present and future collapse – from a God's-eye point of view – into an eternal present. For God, in other words, our

temporal distinctions are meaningless, as He can see everything that has happened and that will happen as if in an eternal present.

Another way that we experience time is through language, so that, in this new and eternal world, Petrarch says: there will be 'no "will be", nor "was", nor "never", nor "before", nor "after", those things that make human life changeable and variable.'[60] The words we use to mark time will have no meaning in this new realm (Petrarch reiterates this viewpoint later in the poem). And yet, those who make it to that eternal realm will have their memories preserved eternally: 'Blessed are those spirits that in the highest chorus' – the celestial chorus of the angels – 'will find or do find themselves at such a level that their names will exist in eternal memory! O, how fortunate is he who brooks this mountainous, fast-running torrent whose name is life and which so many find so pleasing!'[61] Life

– meaning human life on earth – is seen as treacherous terrain, full of pitfalls, a river ever moving that is hazardous to human beings and their potential salvations. Those happy, saved few will have their names preserved in eternity, so that they will experience not the fame of the earthly world, but rather fame that is guaranteed forever.

Like religiously inclined thinkers everywhere who contemplate life beyond earthly existence, Petrarch imagines a realm that is both different from but also fundamentally like that on earth: earth without the problems, as it were. This too is why people on earth are deluded: 'Wretched are the people, common and blind, who place their hopes here on earth in the sorts of things that time so swiftly whisks away.'[62] These are people, in other words, who have not come to realize the way time inflects our lives: every day we seem to live without thinking of death, which is inevitable, and we do not realize

24 Francesco Pesellino, *Triumphs of Love, Chastity, and Death, c.* 1450, tempera and gilt on wood.

that 'one hour breaks apart what it took many years and great effort to gather together.'[63] Only those who make it to heaven and to the time when there is no time will be truly happy, fortunate and blessed, for when they are 'famous once' – in heaven – 'they will be so forever'.[64] In the final analysis and in general terms: 'O how happy are those souls who are or will be on the way to the destination I am talking about, whenever it will occur!'[65] Only eternity will resolve all the vacillation, time-bound activity, and instability that life itself presents.

Yet making this statement is not enough for Petrarch. As he moves to the second half of the poem, we see where his mind turns, indeed where his whole energy must turn, towards the end of his life. He turns, of course, to Laura: 'most blessed is she whom Death struck down far before her natural end!'[66] Laura's early death, from plague, is presented as an advantage to her, since she escaped the world and its miseries. In the

heavenly realm, alongside the angels, 'there will appear the honourable words and chaste thoughts that nature had placed in her heart when young'.[67] Petrarch himself will be there too, turned towards precisely the place where Love had bound him – to Laura. People will look at him and say: 'There is the one who wept continually, who even in his weeping was blessed above the joys of others. And she of whom I sing, even as I keep weeping, will be wonderstruck at her very self, seeing how she is vaunted among all the rest.'[68] Finally, he will be with Laura, his lifelong muse, whose beauty, chastity and womanly perfection never ceased to occasion such emotion ('weeping') on Petrarch's part. Even in heaven she will retain her individuality: her modest nature will be 'wonderstruck' at the fact that she is in such a blessed state.

As to when the moment will occur (the moment, that is, of the Last Judgment and the passage into a timeless realm),

25 Francesco Pesellino, *Triumphs of Fame, Time, and Eternity*, c. 1448, tempera on panel.

Petrarch says: 'I do not know.' But: 'I do believe it is approaching.'[69] Along with that final moment, there will be a reckoning, whereby 'every conscience whether clear or clouded will be open and naked before the world. And there will be One who judges and knows what is right.'[70] In the light of that final judgment, God's judgment, 'we will see each and every person take his journey, like an animal driven towards a cave; and it will be seen how little heritage counts, the sort of heritage that engenders pride, and how gold, and land, instead of being advantages, were really disadvantages.'[71] Those who have sinned, in other words, will be visited with divine vengeance. By the same token, those who have lived modestly and well will be 'set apart' from the damned.[72]

As Petrarch winds to his conclusion, he refers to the previous five Triumphs, all of them superseded by this one, and he restates that the dead will come back and 'will have eternal fame, along with immortal beauty'.[73] Before he concludes, Petrarch needs, one more time, to pay tribute to Laura, even as he links himself (and his writing) to her forever:

> Before all those who are to be remade is the one whom the world, weeping, calls, with my tongue and my tired pen; though heaven too yearns to see her whole. At the bank of a river born in the Cevennes, love bestowed upon me such a long war for her, one that my heart calls to memory even now. What a fortunate stone, that covers that beautiful face. At that time when she will have put back on her veil, if he who saw her on earth was blessed, what will it then be to see her in heaven?[74]

The river to which Petrarch refers is the Durance, a tributary
of the Rhone that runs through Petrarch's beloved Vaucluse
and joins the Rhone near Avignon. The 'stone' signifies
Laura's grave, which seems fortunate to be so close to such
beauty. Finally, there is the 'veil', a common expression denot-
ing the body. In other words, when Laura is resurrected, she
will be almost impossibly beautiful. The culmination of all
the striving and art Petrarch had put into his poetry will be
newly embodied in something perfect, incorruptible and
eternal.

It should be no surprise, nor is it really a reproach against
Petrarch to say it: his feelings about Laura are about Petrarch.
Laura was an abstraction. But it was a sustaining abstraction
for him, one that he kept tenaciously in his mind for his whole
life, and one that emerged in the *Triumph of Eternity*, his last
work. The *Triumph of Eternity* was the ultimate 'if only' moment:
if only he could meet Laura in heaven. If only he could surpass
Dante. If only he could rid himself of his crippling self-doubt,
a doubt that related to life in the world, with its uncertainties,
all tied to time, mundanity, and to humanity's sometimes
crippling physicality. If only.

Epilogue:
Death and Afterlife

AVING SUFFERED ON AND OFF for four years from an affliction that caused fainting, Petrarch died on 19 July 1374. One of his close friends, Giovanni Dondi, was a doctor, and on that day he wrote to another medical friend as follows:

> This unfortunate night that has just passed, which has ceded into this very day on which I am writing you, took from us our renowned and admirable Petrarch. He was struck some hours earlier with that same illness from which he was suffering a few years ago, when you and I went together to visit him in his pleasant refuge in the Euganean Hills.[1]

The 'Euganean Hills'. These small mountains can be seen, just barely, from Venice and are in the general province of Padua, whose rulers, the Carrara family, had offered Petrarch patronage in his final years. Right in the middle of these mountains there is a village called Arquà Petrarca – the same Arquà where Petrarch settled and whose leaders, over time, decided to add the name of its most illustrious inhabitant to its own (illus. 26). Petrarch's fame was great at his death and

became ever more so with the passage of time. Yet the reasons for his fame, along with what people took from his life and work, changed according to time and circumstance.

One reason Petrarch's name was venerated in the immediate years after his death was his gift for friendship. Despite his occasionally testy misanthropy, Petrarch understood his friends, what mattered to them and what they considered meaningful. Petrarch had written a will in 1370, and his concern for his friends emerges clearly there. To his friend Donato Albanzani, for instance (the same Donato to whom he had dedicated *On His Own Ignorance*), Petrarch offers remittance from any debt that might have accrued.[2] Donato would go on to translate Petrarch's *On Illustrious Men* into the vernacular. Donato thus served as a crucial link in the chain that connected Petrarch's Latin classical scholarship to the vernacular

26 The modern-day landscape of Arquà Petrarca.

classicism that became part and parcel of fifteenth-century Italian intellectual life.[3]

Or take what Petrarch bequeathed to Boccaccio in his will: 'To Lord Giovanni of Certaldo, or Boccaccio, though I am ashamed to leave such a modest portion to such a great man, I bequeath fifty Florentine gold florins, for a winter coat for his studies and night-time scholarly work.'[4] The 'florin' was a coin struck by the city of Florence from 1252 onwards, and in the late fourteenth century it was becoming a recognized instrument of trade in Europe. It was prestigious and valuable. Petrarch's gift to Boccaccio was no trifle: it represented the equivalent of roughly one and a half years of wages for an unskilled worker.[5] But it is the way Petrarch couches the gift that is most notable. It is not just money, rather it is a gift 'for a winter coat'. And it is not just any winter coat, but one that can be worn when Boccaccio is engaging in study. Boccaccio was known, despite his aristocratic family heritage, to be far from well off. Petrarch's concern for framing this gift in the right way is touching, deflecting as he does the financial aspect and turning the spirit of the gift instead to the subject they shared and loved: scholarship. Boccaccio was grateful for Petrarch's remembrance, and Boccaccio recognized, too, that the gift represented 'quite an ample portion of goods', as he wrote in a letter to Petrarch's son-in-law.[6]

Those like Boccaccio and Donato Albanzani, who knew Petrarch and loved him as a friend, took care to preserve and transmit Petrarch's work. In that same letter to Petrarch's son-in-law (who was also the executor of Petrarch's will), Boccaccio expresses concern that Petrarch's *Africa* ('a work I consider celestial') might fall into the wrong hands.[7] The

Africa was a work that Petrarch had indeed kept close to his chest, believing that it was never really finished. Boccaccio's fears were justified. The truth was that there was only one definitive version of it, in Petrarch's papers, and everyone knew how fragile the world of manuscripts was. For the *Africa*, especially, but also for other Petrarchan works, there was something like a mad scramble among the next generation, as a number of interested admirers sought to gain access to Petrarch's literary legacy.[8]

Petrarch's zeal for Latin and the ancient world contributed decisively to a growing passion for antiquity, one that reached a fever pitch in Florence. Part of that classicizing trend, among some intellectuals, was a precise and highly developed sense for a classicizing Latin style. They made a priority of striving to write in Latin in such a way that one could be original, on the one hand, but also 'match' the syntax of classic ancient authors, like Cicero, who were all the rage. Petrarch, too, had shared this aspiration. But as thinkers concentrated their energies on Latin style, and as they looked ever more intensely into the classical Latin heritage, they also focused critical attention on the thinkers that had come before them in this new literary, classicizing movement.

Looked at under this lens, Petrarch's Latin began to seem imperfect. Two intellectual generations after Petrarch flourished, a group of intellectuals arose in the city of Florence who represented the vanguard of this refined classicizing tendency. They perfected their classicizing Latin, some of them served the state in an active political way, and all took a thinker's Latin style as a key measure in evaluating that thinker's worth. None was greater in this group than Leonardo

Bruni (1370–1444), who served both as a papal secretary and then, for many years, as chancellor of the city of Florence, one of its highest political positions. Bruni was originally from the Tuscan city of Arezzo, but after arriving in Florence, he considered himself a Florentine first and foremost, winning citizenship and, eventually, a tax exemption for being the city's chief historian.

The greater part of Bruni's efforts in his literary work aimed at celebrating Florence – its institutions, culture and famous personalities. In this latter respect, though Bruni wrote most of his work in Latin, he also wrote biographies, in Tuscan, of Dante and Petrarch. About Petrarch, Bruni wrote that he was

> the first with a talent sufficient to recognize and call back to light the antique elegance of the lost and extinguished style. Admittedly, it was not perfect in him, yet it was he by himself who saw and opened the way to its perfection, for he rediscovered the works of Cicero.[9]

Bruni, in other words, evinced great respect for Petrarch as having been the first thinker definitively to make ancient style something worthwhile for the present. What is more, Bruni was one of the prime movers in associating Petrarch and his memory strongly with Florence. Here and elsewhere, Bruni also criticized Petrarch, as having only imperfectly reached the levels of eloquence in Latin that Bruni's own generation prized. Another thinker, Flavio Biondo (a friend of Bruni's), had a similar opinion:

First of all, Francesco Petrarch, a man of great talent and great industry, began to awaken poetry and eloquence. But in that age in which we blame the dearth and lack of books more than of genius, he did not attain the flower of Ciceronian eloquence that adorns many that we see in this century.[10]

Generations. From this point on – let us say within the lifetime of Bruni, who died in 1444 – there were, in effect, three Petrarchs on whom succeeding generations could fasten. First, there was Petrarch the classicist, who 'stepped into the footsteps of the ancients' and who was well regarded among many Italian intellectuals for having done so. Bruni and his generation fully endorsed this Petrarch: the Petrarch who belittled hyper-specialization, who believed in cultivating eloquence (even if his Latin was never up to snuff in their eyes) and who, importantly, looked towards antiquity to enable a better modernity. Not all Italian thinkers (Bruni included) would embrace Petrarch's linking of classicism and Christianity, but his steadfast belief that the ancient world served as a model for a world today fallen was an inspiration to many. For almost all thinkers in the Italian Renaissance, whatever their orientation, this Petrarch remained a point of pride, a model and a venerated predecessor.[11]

Then there was Petrarch the Latinist, or rather, the scholar and writer who wrote in Latin. This was the Petrarch who, despite his fondest hopes in life, was destined for centuries of relative oblivion. It was not that his Latin works were unknown: with the advent of printing with moveable type, most of his Latin works were gathered together and preserved. It was just that succeeding generations tended to share the judgement of Bruni and his peers. This Petrarch – the Latin writer – would be rediscovered in the late nineteenth century, as Italy searched in ever greater depth for its national literary heritage. And the *Africa*, Petrarch's unfinished Latin epic, enjoyed a noteworthy if unsurprising afterlife during Italy's Fascist period, addressing as it did the potential greatness of Italy and the conquest of part of Africa.[12] Ultimately, in the twentieth century, as scholars interested in the Italian Renaissance came to understand the amount of unstudied Latin material pertaining to that period, Petrarch's Latin work came into view.[13] Still, however, it is known almost exclusively to scholarly specialists in the field.

Finally, there was Petrarch the vernacular poet. It was in this realm of writing that Petrarch had the most direct influence on the intellectual and cultural life of succeeding eras. Moreover, it was this identity that emerged, in modern times, as the most persistent. Paradoxically, part of this development had to do with the fifteenth-century passion for Latin that Petrarch had inspired in the fourteenth century. To put it simply, Italian thinkers concerned with developing the Italian vernacular into a language of permanence, having studied Latin from all angles, came to the conclusion that Tuscan – Petrarch's language – was the variety of Italian best suited to becoming a 'high' language. In the century after his death, Petrarch's Tuscan poetry rose to such a level in Renaissance thinkers' minds that one prominent intellectual, Cristoforo Landino, began teaching courses on Petrarch's sonnets at the University of Florence. In a prefatory lecture to those courses (in the late 1460s), he stressed that any language worthy of

respect needed to have both learning and craft behind it. He
went on, 'since without the Latin language these things cannot
be acquired, whoever wants to be a good Tuscan must first be
a good Latin'.[14] What he meant was that for Tuscan to attain
the level of respect, discipline and agreed-upon rules that
Latin long enjoyed, those interested in developing Tuscan
needed to know classical Latin first and foremost. Petrarch's
Tuscan poetry (and Boccaccio's prose) seemed to many to
embody just that collection of attributes: they combined a
disciplined written structure, capable of being taught, learned
and institutionally preserved, with a natural, spoken eloquence
that could be employed by people who were native speakers.

By the 1520s in Italy, it was as if people were living in a
new world. The Protestant Reformation had begun (though
not everyone realized its far-reaching implications at the
time), and Martin Luther and his growing numbers of followers were vigorously challenging the papacy's supremacy
in all matters Christian. Italy itself was suffering through a
sequence of debilitating wars, having been invaded by various
outside powers, including the French, Spanish and others, and
there seemed no end in sight. Printing with moveable type,
having reached Italy in the 1460s, had become an acknowledged new reality, with books assuming standardized forms
and with book production reaching ever greater heights. This
latter factor, book production, also meant that a sense of information overload began to surface more frequently.[15] In short,
these reasons and more prompted a search for order and
standardization in many realms. In Italy, one of those realms
was language. And there was no more important person on
this front than Pietro Bembo (1470–1547).[16]

Bembo, the son of a prominent Venetian diplomat, had been exposed early on to the Tuscan language, as his father believed it was a necessary complement to a good education. Bembo's experience, accompanying his father, engendered in him a key assumption that all good diplomats share: clear communicative language is essential. Bembo's Latin writing followed the gold standard of classical Ciceronian prose, an enterprise at which he was so accomplished that he was named a papal secretary in 1513. When it came to Italian – and to the question of which variety of Italian was suitable as a high language – there was no question: it was Tuscan, a language for which Bembo had developed a deep love as a boy, when he spent two years in Florence at his father's side. Bembo wrote a well-received work of love poetry in Tuscan and early on began writing what became the most influential text on the Italian language, a dialogue called the *Prose della volgar lingua*, literally, *Writings on the Vernacular Language*.

Petrarch is, quite simply, everywhere in the *Prose*. His works are cited constantly, as examples to be discussed, analysed for proper usage and imitated. It should be said that, in terms of genre, the *Prose* is a dialogue, so different opinions are expressed by different characters. But in the final analysis, the verdict is clear. The best sort of Italian is Tuscan, and the best variety of Tuscan was that perfected in the fourteenth century by Petrarch in poetry, Boccaccio in prose. As one of the interlocutors puts it authoritatively, though there were other Tuscans who came later, 'it is apparent that the great growth of the language was owed alone to these two, Petrarch and Boccaccio. From that point on, no one has even reached their level of achievement, let alone gone beyond it.'[17] Petrarch the

Tuscan poet thus served as one of the cornerstones in the making of modern, standardized Italian. It should be said, too, that the *Prose* manifests one of the rare occasions when one of Petrarch's deep, though always unarticulated, hopes became a reality: he was privileged as a model for poetic language over and above Dante.[18]

Petrarch the poet also served as an inspiring force for many other thinkers and artists in the centuries after his death. In the sixteenth century there was, for example, a relative outpouring of women's writing in Tuscan, as authors like Vittoria Colonna and Veronica Gambara wrote lyric poetry, inspired as much by Petrarch's literary achievement as by the fact that a native language was seen as suitable for serious writing.[19] Across Europe, 'Petrarchism' spread, as French writers like Louise Labé and English writers like Edmund Spenser adapted and transformed Petrarch's lyricism in their own contexts.[20]

Thinkers and artists in the Romantic era were inspired by Petrarch's dreamy, haunted persona, his devotion to an unattainable ideal (in the form of Laura) and his dedication to his poetic craft. This epoch saw Petrarch enter the landscape, as it were, becoming part and parcel of the 'Grand Tour', wherein northern European travellers made their way south to Italy, stirred by its ancient ruins (as Petrarch himself had been) and seeking ever deeper connections to its culture. The poet Percy Bysshe Shelley (1792–1822) can stand as one example, and there is no better poem in which to see these tendencies than his 'Lines Written among the Euganean Hills'. The Euganean Hills, of course, represented the place where Petrarch had found his final home, in Arquà. For

Shelley, mentally recovering after the recent death of his daughter Clara, a stay there led to a meditation on time, death, and nature, one in which poets had their place. He dedicated a number of lines within the poem to his friend Lord Byron, writing:

> As the ghost of Homer clings
> Round Scamander's wasting springs;
> As divinest Shakespeare's
> Fills Avon and the world with light
> Like omniscient power which he
> Imag'd 'mid mortality;
> As the love from Petrarch's urn
> Yet amid yon hills doth burn,
> A quenchless lamp by which the heart
> Sees things unearthly; so thou art,
> Mighty spirit: so shall be
> The City that did refuge thee. (ll.194–205).

Writing is linked to place: that of Homer to the Scamander River, that of Shakespeare to Avon and beyond, and that of Petrarch to the Euganean Hills. Petrarch's love for Laura becomes a 'quenchless lamp' that will forever burn in the hills and that permits one to see 'things unearthly'. Venice, the unnamed 'City', will be to Byron what those other geographies were and are to their respective poets.

Later, in the realm of music, the composer and performer Franz Liszt (1811–1886) set three of Petrarch's sonnets to music.[21] One of them is worth quoting extensively, if not entirely: 'I find no peace and am done with war; and I fear, and I hope; I am burning up, and I am frozen; and I fly above the heavens, and lie down on the earth; nothing do I hold dear, and I embrace the whole world.'[22] This is also Shelley's Petrarch, who flies 'above the heavens' to see things of which the earthbound can only dream. Petrarch goes on: 'Without eye do I see, without tongue do I wail; I want to die, yet I ask for help; I hold myself in hatred, and I love another. I feed on grief, I cry as I laugh; and death and life please me in equal measure: I am in this state, Lady, for you.'[23] Here is Petrarch in full, his love for Laura symbolizing so much more: his interiority versus his exteriority, his emotional back and forth between extreme joy and the depths of despair, and his mesmeric fascination with life, death and what lies beyond.

Liszt originally set the words of this and two other poems to music. He later reconfigured the project and integrated the piano score into the second volume of his *Years of Pilgrimage*, a kind of artistic, multimedia version of the Grand Tour. This volume covered Italy, and in it music, art and literature all stood side by side, with Raphael, Michelangelo, the Baroque painter and poet Salvator Rosa, Petrarch and Dante all having inspired Lisztian compositions. Each was represented by his work: a painting for Raphael, a sculpture for Michelangelo, three sonnets of Petrarch and, finally, the *Divine Comedy* of Dante.[24] Dante was last and – one has the sense from the number of times Liszt mentioned or wrote work inspired by Dante – most important. As in life, so also in death, at least in this case: Dante held first place, Petrarch second.

There are an infinite number of ways to trace Petrarch's fortunes and reputation in the centuries after his death. This is neither the place nor the time to do so. So the best way to

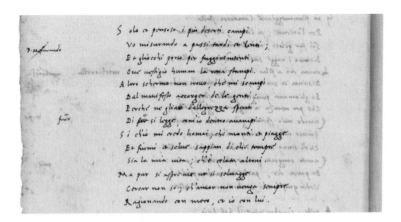

conclude is to listen once more to Petrarch, to one of his most affecting poems, one that was later set to music by both Haydn and Schubert, called 'Solo et pensoso' (and one that, as it happens, Bembo had copied out by hand (illus. 27):

Solo et pensoso i più deserti campi
vo mesurando a passi tardi et lenti,
et gli occhi porto per fuggire intenti
ove vestigio human l'arena stampi.

Alone and thoughtful through the most deserted fields I go, with slow, uncertain steps, and I direct my eyes to avoid any place human footsteps mark the sand.

Altro schermo non trovo che mi scampi
dal manifesto accorger de le genti,
perché negli atti d'alegrezza spenti
di fuor si legge com'io dentro avampi:

27 Bembo's handwritten transcript of Petrarch's poem 'Solo et pensoso' from his *Canzoniere*, 1502.

I find no defence that can protect me from people's
open notice, since in my quenched aspect of joy, from
outside one reads how I burn within.

Sì ch'io mi credo omai che monti et piagge
et fiumi et selve sappian di che tempre
sia la mia vita, chè celata altrui.

So it is that I now believe that mountains and river-
banks and rivers and woods know the quality of my
life, which from others is hidden.

Ma pur sí aspre vie né sí selvagge
cercar non so ch'Amor non venga sempre
ragionando con meco, et io con lui.[25]

But I know I cannot find roads so harsh or wild that
Love would not come and converse with me, and I
with him.

Petrarch likely wrote this poem when he was in his early thir-
ties, a young man with some achievements behind him and
many more to come.

It is striking how, even here, even in the artifice-inflected
realm of poetry, which is bound by meter and allusive language, Petrarch knows himself: he knows that he has this
tendency to withdraw from human contact, he is aware that
his inner turmoil is visible from without, and he is cognizant
of the fact that he will always be on the lookout for the inspiration of 'Love', something that we know by now is as much a

never-to-be-realized aspiration as it is a reality. Perhaps his strongest legacy today, then, is that this remarkably inner-oriented man found ways throughout his life to turn outwards, to seek fame and glory, and to leave his identity, his personality, so clearly behind. Private yet public, friendly yet irascible, looking ever backwards yet dreaming of the future, Petrarch's personal complexity, so openly revealed, makes him a figure of endless fascination and one that speaks to our age more than ever.

REFERENCES

1 Origins and Early Years

1 Francesco Petrarch, ed. and trans. Gianni Villani, *Lettera ai Posteri* (Rome, 1990), p. 34.
2 Ibid., p. 42.
3 Armando Petrucci, ed. and trans. Charles M. Radding, *Writers and Readers in Medieval Italy* (New Haven, CT, 1995).
4 Kenneth J. Pratt, 'Rome as Eternal', *Journal of the History of Ideas*, XXVI (1965), pp. 25–44.
5 Michele Maccarrone, *Vicarius Christi: Storia del titolo papale* (Rome, 1952).
6 See Matthew 16:18 and Eamon Duffy, *Saints and Sinners: A History of the Popes* (New Haven, CT, 1997), pp. 1–132.
7 The document is cited in Ernst Hatch Wilkins, *Studies in the Life and Works of Petrarch* (Cambridge, MA, 1955), pp. 6–7; see also Ernst Hatch Wilkins, *Life of Petrarch* (Chicago, 1961), p. 11.
8 See Arthur Field, *The Origins of the Platonic Academy* (Princeton, NJ, 1988), pp. 26–7.
9 Francesco Petrarch, trans. Aldo Bernardo, *Letters of Old Age* (New York, 2005), 10.2, p. 362.
10 Francesco Petrarch, ed. and trans. Otto and Eva Schönberger, *Epistulae metricae / Briefe in Versen* (Würzburg, 2004), 1.7, p. 82, ll. 30 and 38.
11 Francesco Petrarch, ed. Vittorio Rossi and trans. Ugo Dotti, *Le familiari: Familiarum rerum libri* (Racconigi, 2004–9), 10.3, vol. II, p. 1376.
12 Petrarch, *Letters*, 10.2, p. 362.

13 Petrarch, *Lettera*, p. 34.

14 MS Paris, Bibliothèque nationale, Par. Lat., 2923, f. 178v–179r; cf.
    Pierre de Nolhac, *Pétrarque et l'humanisme* (Paris, 1907), vol. II, p. 287;
    Hans Baron, *Petrarch's 'Secretum': Its Making and Meaning* (Cambridge,
    MA, 1985), pp. 23–6.

15 Ugo Dotti, *Vita di Petrarca* (Rome, 2004), p. 6.

16 *Seniles* 16.1, in Francisci Petrarchae *Opera Latina* (Venice, 1503),
    unpaginated.

17 MS Milan, Biblioteca Ambrosiana, A 79 inf., olim Sala del prefetto
    10/27.

18 Giuseppe Billanovich, 'Il Virgilio di Petrarca. Da Avignone a
    Milano', *Studi Petrarcheschi*, n.s./2 (1985), pp. 15–52.

19 Michele Feo, 'Petrarca, Francesco', in *Enciclopedia virgiliana* (Rome,
    1984–8), vol. IV, pp. 53–78.

20 Marco Petoletti, '"Petrus Parentis Florentinus, qui hoc modo
    volume instituit": il codice', in Francesco Petrarch, *Le postille del
    Virgilio Ambrosiano*, ed. Marco Baglio, Antonietta Nebuloni Testa,
    and Marco Petoletti (Rome and Padua, 2006), vol. I, pp. 6–29.

21 Petrarch, *Le postille del Virgilio Ambrosiano*, I:274.

22 Ibid.

23 Aristotle, *Metaphysics*, 12.10.1076a4–5.

24 Cicero, *De natura deorum*, 2.31.79; ibid., 2.35.90; Cicero, *De inventione*,
    1.29.46.

25 Francesco Petrarch, ed. Vittorio Rossi, *Le familiari* (Florence,
    1933–68; re-edition, 1997), 22.2, p. 106.

26 *Eclogues* 6, 54.

27 Giuseppe Billanovich, *La tradizione del testo di Livio e le origini
    dell'umanesimo* (Padua, 1981–), vol. I, p. 187.

28 Petrarch, *Lettera*, p. 46.

29 Petrarch, *Epistulae metricae*, 3.19.16.

30 An English translation can be found in Leonardo Bruni, *The
    Humanism of Leonardo Bruni: Selected Texts*, ed. and trans. Gordon
    Griffiths, James Hankins and David Thompson (Binghamton, NY,
    1987), pp. 95–8.

31 Ibid., p. 97.

32 Petrarch, ed. Rossi, *Le familiari*, 10.3, vol. II, p. 1392.

33 Nolhac, vol. II, pp. 286–7; Dotti, *Vita*, pp. 54–5.

34   See Ovid, *Metamorphoses*, 1:452–567.
35   Ibid., 1:527–30.
36   Ibid., 1:546.
37   Francesco Petrarch, ed. Sabrina Stroppa, *Canzoniere* (Turin, 2011),
     211, p. 353.
38   Ibid.
39   Ibid.

2 The Discovery of the Ancient World

 1   Francesco Petrarch, ed. Vittorio Rossi, *Le familiari* (Florence,
     1933–68; re-edition Florence, 1997), 24.8.
 2   Ibid.
 3   See Giuseppe Billanovich, *La tradizione del testo di Livio e le origini
     dell'umanesimo* (Padua, 1981–); Ugo Dotti, *Vita di Petrarca* (Rome,
     2004), pp. 26–7.
 4   *Seniles* 16.1, in *Francisci Petrarchae Opera Latina* (Venice, 1503),
     unpaginated; an English translation of the letter can be found
     in Francesco Petrarch, *Letters of Old Age*, trans. Aldo Bernardo
     (New York, 2005), pp. 599–607.
 5   Ibid.
 6   Cicero, *Pro Archia*, 2.
 7   Ibid., p. 3.
 8   Aulus Gellius, *Noctes Atticae*, 13.17.
 9   See Paul Oskar Kristeller, *Renaissance Thought and its Sources*
     (New York, 1979).
10   Petrarch, *Le familiari*, 6.2.
11   Francesco Petrarch, ed. Vittorio Rossi and trans. Ugo Dotti,
     Le familiari: Familiarum rerum libri (Racconigi, 2004–9), 4.1, vol. 1,
     pp. 468–86.
12   Ibid., p. 468.
13   Ibid., p. 474.
14   Ibid., p. 476.
15   Ovid, *Amores*, 3.11.35.
16   Petrarch, *Le familiari: Familiarum*, 4.1, vol. 1, p. 482.
17   Ibid. See Augustine, *Confessions*, 10.8.15.
18   Petrarch, *Le familiari: Familiarum*, 4.1, vol. 1, p. 482.

19 Ibid., pp. 484–6.
20 Francesco Petrarch, ed. and trans. Gianni Villani, *Lettera ai posteri* (Rome, 1990), p. 50.
21 Ibid.
22 Petrarch, *Le familiari: Familiarum*, 2.12, vol. I, p. 286.
23 Ibid., pp. 284–6.
24 Ibid., p. 286.
25 Petrarch, *Le familiari: Familiarum*, 2.13, vol. I, p. 292.
26 Ibid., 2.14, vol. I, p. 294.
27 Francesco Petrarch, ed. Sabrina Stroppa, *Canzoniere* (Turin, 2011), 53, pp. 104–6.
28 Ibid., p. 104; Francesco Petrarch, ed. and trans. Robert M. Durling, *Petrarch's Lyric Poems* (Cambridge, MA, 1978).
29 Ibid.
30 Ibid.
31 Ibid., p. 104; trans. Durling, modified, p. 126.
32 Petrarch, *Canzoniere*, 53, p. 105; Petrarch, *Petrarch's Lyric*, p. 126.
33 Petrarch, *Canzoniere*, 53, p.105; Petrarch, *Petrarch's Lyric*, p. 128.

3 A Reputation Assured

1 *De vita solitaria*, 2.15, in Francesco Petrarch, ed. Giuseppe Martellotti, *Prose* (Milan, 1955), pp. 286–591, at p. 582.
2 Francesco Petrarch, ed. and trans. Gianni Villani, *Lettera ai posteri* (Rome, 1990), pp. 50–52.
3 Petrarch, *Lettera*, pp. 52–4.
4 Francesco Petrarch, ed. Vittorio Rossi, *Le familiari* (Florence, 1933–68; re-edition Florence, 1997), 4.1–4.8.
5 See Dante, *Paradiso*, 25, 1–12; Ernest Hatch Wilkins, 'The Coronation of Petrarch', *Speculum*, XVIII (1943), pp. 155–97.
6 Petrarch, *Le familiari*, 4.6.
7 Petrarch, *Lettera*, p. 54.
8 See Francesco Petrarch, ed. Giulio Cesare Maggi, *La Collatio laureationis* (Milan, 2012); there is an annotated English translation in Ernest Hatch Wilkins, *Studies in the Life and Works of Petrarch* (Cambridge, MA, 1955), pp. 300–313.
9 Virgil, *Georgics*, 3.291–92.

10 See Dennis Looney, 'The Beginnings of Humanistic Oratory:
    Petrarch's *Coronation Oration* (*Collatio laureationis*)', in *Petrarch: A Critical
    Guide to the Complete Works*, ed. Victoria Kirkham and Armando
    Maggi (Chicago, IL, 2009), pp. 131–40.

11 Ibid., p. 135.

12 Ernst Hatch Wilkins, 'The Coronation', in Ernst Hatch Wilkins,
    Life of Petrarch (Chicago, 1961), p. 188; Wilkins, *Life*, p. 28.

13 Francesco Petrarch, ed. Giuseppe Martellotti, *Prose*, p. 218.

14 See Ronald G. Musto, *Apocalypse in Rome: Cola di Rienzo and the Politics
    of the New Age* (Berkeley, Los Angeles and London, 2003).

15 *Cronica*, ed. Giuseppe Porta (Milan, 1979), ch. 18.

16 Petrarch, *Epistolae variae*, 43, ed. in *Briefwechsel des Cola di Rienzo*, vol.
    II in Konrad Burdach and Paul Piur, *Vom Mittelalter zur Reformation*,
    5 parts (Berlin: Weidemann, 1913–29), 2: 2.3: 63–81; English
    translation in *The Revolution of Cola di Rienzo*, ed. Ronald G. Musto
    and trans. Mario Emilio Cosenza (New York, 1996), pp. 10–24,
    at p. 18.

17 *The Revolution of Cola di Rienzo*, p. 16.

18 Ibid., pp. 16–17.

19 Ibid., p. 17.

20 Ibid.

21 Ibid.

22 Ibid., p. 18.

23 Ibid.

24 Ibid., p. 20.

25 Ibid., p. 21.

26 Ibid., p. 23.

27 Francesco Petrarch, ed. Sabrina Stroppa, *Canzoniere* (Turin, 2011), I,
    p. 3.

28 Francesco Petrarch, ed. and trans. Robert M. Durling, *Petrarch's Lyric
    Poems* (Cambridge, MA, 1978), p. 36.

29 See Ugo Dotti, *Vita di Petrarca* (Rome, 2004), pp. 53–8.

30 Latin cited in Dotti, *Vita di Petrarca*, p. 54.

31 Petrarch, *Canzoniere*, 211, p. 353.

32 Petrarch, *Petrarch's Lyric*, p. 364.

33 Petrarch, *Canzoniere*, 128, p. 240.

34 Ibid.

35 Ibid.
36 Ibid.
37 Ibid.
38 Ibid.
39 Ibid., p. 241.
40 Ibid.
41 Ibid., p. 242.
42 James Hankins has developed this theme; see his 'Teaching Civil
    Prudence in Leonardo Bruni's *History of the Florentine People*', in *Ethik
    – Wissenschaft oder Lebenskunst? Modelle der Normenbegründung von der
    Antike bis zur frühen Neuzeit*, ed. Sabrina Ebbersmeyer and Eckhard
    Kessler (Berlin, 2007), pp. 143–57.
43 Petrarch, *Canzoniere*, 128, p. 242.
44 Latin text cited in Pierre de Nolhac, *Pétrarque et l'humanisme*
    (Paris, 1907), vol. II, p. 284.

4 The Interior Man

1 See Ronald G. Witt, 'Introduction', in Francesco Petrarch, ed. and
   trans. Susan S. Schearer, *On Religious Leisure* (New York, 2002), pp.
   ix–xxv, at p. ix; Gherardo had become a *renditus*, meaning someone
   who took the vows of chastity, poverty and obedience but was not
   obligated to live in the cloister; see also Ugo Dotti, *Vita di Petrarca*
   (Rome, 2004), pp. 151–4.
2 Latin text in Francesco Petrarch, ed. Antonietta Bufano, *Opere latine*
   (Turin, 1975), vol. I, pp. 568–808, at p. 568; Petrarch, *On Religious
   Leisure*, p. 3.
3 Petrarch, *Opere latine*, vol. I, p. 572; Petrarch, *On Religious Leisure*, p. 5.
4 Petrarch, *Opere latine*, vol. I, p. 652; Petrarch, *On Religious Leisure*, p. 56.
5 Petrarch, *Opere latine*, vol. I, p. 654; Petrarch, *On Religious Leisure*, p. 56.
6 Petrarch, *Opere latine*, vol. I, p. 656; Petrarch, *On Religious Leisure*, p. 57.
7 Petrarch, *Opere latine*, vol. I, p. 658; Petrarch, *On Religious Leisure*, p. 58.
8 See *Pestilential Complexities: Understanding Medieval Plague*, ed. Vivian
   Nutton (London, 2008); Philip Ziegler, *The Black Death* (London,
   1969); John Aberth, *From the Brink of the Apocalypse: Confronting Famine,
   War, Plague, and Death in the Later Middle Ages*, 2nd edn (London,
   2009), pp. 79–213; for a different view, see Samuel K. Cohn, Jr,

The Black Death Transformed: Disease and Culture in Early Renaissance Europe
(London, 2003).

9   Giovanni Boccaccio, trans. Wayne Rebhorn, *Decameron*
(New York, 2015), p. 4.

10 Ibid.

11 Ibid.

12 Ibid.

13 Ibid., p. 6.

14 Ibid.

15 Ibid.

16 Ibid.

17 Ibid., p. 8.

18 Ibid., p. 11.

19 See Wayne Rebhorn, 'Introduction', in Boccaccio, *Decameron*,
pp. xxiii–lxvi, at p. xxiii.

20 Pierre de Nolhac, *Pétrarque et l'humanisme* (Paris, 1907) vol. II, p. 286.

21 Ibid., vol. II, pp. 286–7.

22 For the negative associations of Babylon, see Genesis 11; Revelation
17:5.

23 Francesco Petrarch, ed. Vittorio Rossi and trans. Ugo Dotti,
Le familiari: Familiarum rerum libri (Racconigi, 2004–9), 7.7., vol. II,
p. 948.

24 See Theodore J. Cachey, Jr., 'Poetry in Motion', in *The Cambridge
Companion to Petrarch*, ed. Albert Ascoli and Unn Falkeid
(Cambridge, 2015), pp. 13–25.

25 Francesco Petrarch, ed. and trans. Bernhard Huss and Gerhard
Regn, *Secretum meum* (Mainz, 2004), p. 18.

26 Augustine, *Confessions*, 2.1.

27 Rom., 13.13–4.

28 Augustine, *Confessions*, 8.12.

29 It is in the University of Padua Library as MS 1490; see Dotti, *Vita*,
p. 21.

30 Petrarch, *Secretum meum*, p. 12.

31 Ibid., p. 36.

32 Ibid., p. 110.

33 Ibid., p. 228.

34 Ibid., p. 230.

35 Ibid., p. 250.
36 Ibid., p. 256–8.
37 Ibid., p. 266.
38 Ibid.
39 Ibid., p. 270.
40 Ibid., p. 280.
41 Ibid., p. 282.
42 Dotti, *Vita*, p. 54.
43 *Canz.* 77, trans. in Francesco Petrarch, ed. and trans. Robert M. Durling, *Petrarch's Lyric Poems* (Cambridge, MA, 1978), modified. The other mention is in *Canz.* 78.
44 Petrarch, *Secretum meum*, p. 282.
45 Ibid., pp. 292–4.
46 Ibid., p. 298.
47 See Pierre Hadot, *Philosophy as a Way of Life: Spiritual Exercises from Socrates to Foucault* (Oxford, 1995).
48 See Gur Zak, *Petrarch's Humanism and the Care of the Self* (Cambridge, 2010).
49 Petrarch, *Secretum meum*, p. 300.
50 Ibid., p. 310.
51 This was in a Latin 'Metrical letter' to a friend named Ildebrandino Conti; Francesco Petrarch, ed. and trans. Otto and Eva Schönberger, *Epistulae metricae / Briefe in Versen* (Würzburg, 2004), 3.25.
52 Petrarch, *Secretum meum*, p. 312.
53 Ibid., p. 324.
54 Ibid.
55 Ibid., p. 334.
56 Ibid.
57 Ibid., p. 340.
58 See Pierre Hadot, *The Inner Citadel: The 'Meditations' of Marcus Aurelius* (Cambridge, MA, 2001).
59 The 'long' and 'short' versions of Petrarch's preface are translated in Benjamin J. Kohl, 'Petrarch's Prefaces to *De Viris Illustribus*', *History and Theory*, XIII (1974), pp. 132–44, pp. 138–42, pp. 142–4, at p. 138.
60 Ibid., p. 139.

61 See *Sen.* 9.1, edited in Emanuele Casamassima, 'L'autografo della
    seconda lettera del Petrarca a Urbino V (*Senile* IX 1)', *Quaderni
    petrarcheschi*, III (1985–6), pp. 103–34, p. 116; and Silvia Rizzo,
    Ricerche sul latino umanistico (Rome, 2002), p. 37.

62 Albertino Mussato, ed. Luigi Padrin, *Ecerinide: Tragedia* (Bologna,
    1900); see Ronald G. Witt, *In the Footsteps of the Ancients: The Origins
    of Humanism from Lovato to Bruni* (Leiden, 2003), pp. 118–29.

63 Petrarch, *Africa*, 9.9–97.

64 Ibid., 9. 97–102.

65 Henri de Lubac, *Exégèse médiévale: les quatre sens de l'Écriture* (Paris, 1959–).

66 Petrarch, *Africa*, 9.136–8.

67 Ibid., 9.147.

68 Ibid., 9.216–21.

69 Ibid., 9.221–6.

70 Ibid., 9.249–56.

71 Virgil, *Georgics*, 3.291–2.

72 Petrarch, *Africa*, p. 348; alluding to Cicero, *Pro Marcello*, 8.26.

73 Petrarch, *Africa*, p. 350.

74 Ibid.

75 Ibid., pp. 352–4.

76 Ibid., p. 354.

77 Ibid., p. 376.

78 Ibid., p. 384.

79 Ibid.

80 Ibid., p. 398.

81 Ibid., p. 400.

82 Francesco Petrarch, *Epistulae metricae*, 24, ll. 1–10.

5 A Life in Letters: Petrarch and Boccaccio

1 Francesco Petrarch, ed. and trans. Otto and Eva Schönberger,
   Epistulae metricae / Briefe in Versen (Würzburg, 2004), 3.19, ll. 15–16.

2 Francesco Petrarch, ed. Vittorio Rossi, *Le familiari* (Florence,
   1933–68; re-edition Florence, 1997), 21.5; Latin text consulted in
   Francesco Petrarch, ed. Giuseppe Martellotti, *Prose* (Milan, 1955),
   pp. 1002–14, at p. 1002.

3 Ibid., p. 1004.

4 Ibid.

5 Ibid., p. 1006.

6 Ibid.

7 Ibid.

8 Ibid.

9 Petrarch, *Le familiari*, 22.2, vol. IV, pp. 104–9, at p. 105.

10 Ibid., p. 106.

11 Ibid.

12 Ibid.

13 Ibid.

14 Ibid.

15 Ibid., p. 109.

16 Ibid.

17 Francesco Petrarch, ed. Silvia Rizzo with Monica Berté, *Res seniles*, Libri V–VIII (Florence, 2009), 5.2, pp. 30–51, at p. 32.

18 Ibid.

19 Ibid.

20 Ibid., p. 34.

21 Ibid.

22 Ibid.

23 Ibid., p. 36.

24 Ibid.

25 Ibid.

26 Ibid.

27 Ibid., p. 38.

28 The 'three crowns' were depicted together often and mentioned as such in Giovanni Gherardo da Prato's 1426 *Paradiso degli Alberti.* See Victoria Kirkham, 'Le Tre corone e l'iconografia di Boccaccio', in M. Marchiaro and S. Zamponi, *Boccaccio letterato* (Florence, 2015), pp. 453–84.

29 Petrarch, *Res seniles*, ed. Rizzo, p. 38.

30 Ibid., p. 40.

31 Ibid., p. 42.

32 Ibid.

33 Ibid.

34 Ibid.

35 Ibid., pp. 42–4.

36 Ibid., p. 44.
37 Ibid.
38 Ibid.
39 Ibid.
40 Ibid., p. 46.
41 Ibid.
42 Ibid.
43 The passage the visitor alluded to was Paul, 2 Timothy, 1:12.
44 Ibid., p. 48.
45 Ibid.
46 Dante, *Inferno*, 4.144; on Averroes, see Olivier Leaman, *Averroes and his Philosophy*, 2nd edn (Richmond, Surrey, 1998).
47 See Aristotle, *De anima*, 2.1.412b.
48 Aristotle, *De anima*, 3.4–5.429a10–430a25.
49 See Luca Bianchi, *Il vescovo e i filosofi: La condanna parigina del 1277 e l'evoluzione dell'aristotelismo scolastico* (Bergamo, 1990).

6 Endings

1 Francesco Petrarch, ed. Sabrina Stroppa, *Canzoniere* (Turin, 2011), 142, pp. 7–9.
2 Ibid., 142.13.
3 Ibid., 142.25.
4 Ibid., 142.37–9.
5 Ibid., 136.1; see *Rev.*, 17.
6 Ibid., 136.3–6.
7 Ibid., 136.8–9.
8 Ibid., 136.14.
9 Francesco Petrarch, ed. Ugo Dotti, *Liber sine nomine* (Torino, 2010).
10 There were three printed editions in fifteenth century, nine in the sixteenth and eight in the first half of the seventeenth, as Dotti points out (Ugo Dotti, *Vita di Petrarca* (Rome, 2004), p. 296).
11 Latin text in Francesco Petrarch, ed. and trans. Cristophe Carraud, *Les remèdes aux deux fortunes / De remediis utriusque fortunae, 1354–1366* (Grenoble, 2002).
12 Ibid., 1.15, p. 72.
13 Ibid., 2.92, pp. 946–8.

14 MS Berlin, Staatsbibliothek, Hamilton, 493, and MS Vatican City, Biblioteca apostolica vaticana, Vat. Lat. 3359.

15 Francesco Petrarch, ed. and trans. David Marsh, *Invectives* (Cambridge, MA, 2004), p. 77.

16 Ibid., pp. 168–9.

17 It is *Sen.* 13.5, and is included in Petrarch, *Invectives*.

18 Petrarch, *Invectives*, p. 223.

19 Angelo Poliziano, ed. and trans. Christopher S. Celenza, *Lamia, Angelo Poliziano's Lamia in Context: Text, Translation, and Introductory Studies* (Leiden: Brill, 2010), pp. 194–253, at pp. 194–5.

20 Hannah H. Gray, 'Renaissance Humanism: The Pursuit of Eloquence', *Journal of the History of Ideas*, XXIV (1963), pp. 497–514.

21 Petrarch, *Invectives*, p. 233.

22 Ibid., p. 235.

23 Ibid., p. 239.

24 Ibid.

25 Ibid., p. 239, translation slightly modified.

26 George Sarton, 'Science in the Renaissance', in J. W. Thompson, G. Rowley, F. Schevill and G. Sarton, *The Civilization of the Renaissance* (Chicago, IL, 1929), pp. 79 and 94.

27 Petrarch, *Invectives*, pp. 239–41.

28 See *Universities in the Middle Ages*, vol. I, in *A History of the University in Europe*, ed. Hilde DeRidder-Symoens (Cambridge, 1992); and Marsha Colish, *Medieval Foundations of the Western Intellectual Tradition* (New Haven, CT, 1997), pp. 265–73.

29 Petrarch, *Invectives*, p. 265, modified.

30 Ibid., p. 265, modified.

31 Ibid., p. 265, modified.

32 See Cicero, *De natura deorum*, 1.10.

33 As related in Cicero, *Tusculan Disputations*, 5.3.9.

34 Petrarch, *Invectives*, p. 265.

35 Dante, *Inferno*, 4.131–4.

36 Petrarch, *Invectives*, p. 311.

37 Ibid.

38 David Lines, 'Humanism and the Universities', in *Humanism and Creativity in the Italian Renaissance*, ed. Christopher S. Celenza and Kenneth Gouwens (Leiden, 2006), pp. 323–42.

39 See Daniel Hobbins, 'The Schoolman as Public Intellectual: Jean
    Gerson and the Late Medieval Tract', *American Historical Review*,
    CVIII (2003), pp. 1308–37.

40 Michel de Montaigne, ed. Pier Villey and V. L. Saulnier, *Les essais*
    (Paris, 2004), 3.II, p. 1029.

41 Aristotle, *Nicomachean Ethics*, 2.1–2, 1103a14–1104b3.

42 Petrarch, *Invectives*, p. 312.

43 Ibid., p. 314, modified.

44 Ibid., p. 314, modified.

45 Ibid., p. 320.

46 Augustine, *City of God*, 8.9.

47 Petrarch, *Invectives*, p. 326.

48 Ibid., pp. 344–5.

49 Nereo Vianello, 'I libri di Petrarca e la prima idea di una pubblica
    biblioteca a Venezia', in *Miscellanea marciana di studi bessareonei (a
    coronamento del V Centenario della donazione nicena)* (Padua, 1976), pp.
    435–51.

50 Riccardo Fubini, trans. Martha King, *Humanism and Secularization:
    From Petrarch to Valla* (Durham, NC, 2003); for a different view, see
    Francesco Bausi, *Petrarca Antimoderno* (Florence, 2008).

51 Text in Francesco Petrarch, ed. Emilio Bigi, *Opere di Francesco Petrarca*
    (Milan, 1963), pp. 267–328.

52 *Triumphus fame*, 1.9, in Petrarch, *Opere*, p. 298.

53 *Triumphus temporis*, 32–3 and 61, in Petrarch, *Opere*, pp. 310 and 311.

54 Ibid., 142–5, in Petrarch, *Opere*, p. 313.

55 1 Corinthians 15:20–23.

56 *Triumphus eternitatis*, 1–18, in Petrarch, *Opere*, p. 314.

57 Ibid., 20–21, in Petrarch, *Opere*, p. 314.

58 Revelation 22:1.

59 *Triumphus eternitatis*, 28–31, in Petrarch, *Opere*, p. 314.

60 Ibid., 32–3, in Petrarch, *Opere*, p. 314.

61 Ibid., 43–8, in Petrarch, *Opere*, p. 315.

62 Ibid., 51–2, in Petrarch, *Opere*, p. 315.

63 Ibid., 62–3, in Petrarch, *Opere*, p. 315.

64 Ibid., 80–81, in Petrarch, *Opere*, p. 316.

65 Ibid., 82–4, in Petrarch, *Opere*, p. 316.

66 Ibid., 86–7, in Petrarch, *Opere*, p. 316.

67 Ibid., 88–90, in Petrarch, *Opere*, p. 316.

68 Ibid., 92–9, in Petrarch, *Opere*, p. 316.

69 Ibid., 100 and 103, in Petrarch, *Opere*, p. 316.

70 Ibid., 109–11, in Petrarch, *Opere*, p. 316.

71 Ibid., 114–17, in Petrarch, *Opere*, p. 316.

72 Ibid., 118, in Petrarch, *Opere*, p. 317.

73 Ibid., 134, in Petrarch, *Opere*, p. 317.

74 Ibid., 135–45, in Petrarch, *Opere*, p. 317.

Epilogue: Death and Afterlife

1 Cited in Ugo Dotti, *Vita di Petrarca* (Rome, 2004), p. 439. See also Benjamin J. Kohl, 'Mourners of Petrarch', in *Francis Petrarch: Six Centuries Later: A Symposium*, ed. Aldo Scaglione (Chapel Hill, NC, 1975), pp. 340–52.

2 Francesco Petrarch, 'Testament', in *Petrarch's Testament*, ed. Theodor Mommsen (Ithaca, NY, 1957), pp. 68–93, at pp. 80–81.

3 Most recently, David Lines, 'Beyond Latin in Renaissance Philosophy: A Plea for New Critical Perspectives', *Intellectual History Review*, XXV (2015), pp. 373–89.

4 *Petrarch's Testament*, p. 82.

5 Cf. Richard Goldthwaite, *The Economy of Renaissance Florence* (Baltimore, MD, 2009), table A1.

6 Giovanni Boccaccio, 1374 letter to Francesco da Brossano, in *Giovanni Boccaccio*, ed. Aldo Francesco Massera, *Opere latine minori* (Bari, 1928), pp. 222–7, at p. 226.

7 Ibid.

8 Aldo S. Bernardo, *Petrarch, Scipio, and the* Africa: *The Birth of Humanism's Dream* (Baltimore, MD, 1962), pp. 168–76.

9 Trans. in Gordon Griffiths, James Hankins, and David Thomson, *The Humanism of Leonardo Bruni* (Binghamton, NY, 1987), p. 97.

10 Biondo Flavio, *Italia illustrata*, 6.26, cit. and trans. in Ronald Witt, *In the Footsteps of the Ancients* (Leiden, 2003), p. 340.

11 See Timothy Kircher, 'Petrarch and the Humanists', in *The Cambridge Companion to Petrarch*, ed. Albert Russell Ascoli and Unn Falkeid (Cambridge, 2015), pp. 179–90.

12 Bernardo, *Petrarch, Scipio, and the* Africa (Baltimore, MD, 1962), pp. 168–76.

13 See Christopher S. Celenza, *The Lost Italian Renaissance: Humanists, Historians, and Latin's Legacy* (Baltimore, MD, 2004).

14 Cristoforo Landino, 'Orazione fatta per Cristofano da Pratovecchio quando cominciò a leggere i sonetti di messere Francesco Petrarca in istudio', in R. Cardini, *La critica del Landino* (Florence, 1973), pp. 342–54, at pp. 349–550.

15 Ann Blair, *Too Much to Know: Managing Scholarly Information before the Modern Age* (New Haven, CT, 2011).

16 Stefano Jossa, 'Bembo and Italian Petrarchism', in *The Cambridge Companion to Petrarch*, eds. Albert Russell Ascoli and Unn Falkeid (Cambridge, 2015), pp. 191–200.

17 Pietro Bembo, *Prose della volgar lingua*, 2.2, in Pietro Bembo, ed. Carlo Dionisotti, *Prose della volgar lingua, Gli Asolani, Rime* (Turin, 1966).

18 Jossa, 'Bembo', p. 193.

19 See Virginia Cox, *Women's Writing in Italy, 1400–1650* (Baltimore, MD, 2008); and Ann Rosalind Jones, 'Female Petrarchists', in *The Cambridge Companion to Petrarch*, ed. Albert Russell Ascoli and Unn Falkeid (Cambridge, 2015), pp. 201–9.

20 See William J. Kennedy, *Authorizing Petrarch* (Ithaca, NY, 1994); idem., 'Iberian, French, and English Petrarchisms', in *The Cambridge Companion to Petrarch*, ed. Albert Russell Ascoli and Unn Falkeid (Cambridge, 2015), pp. 210–18.

21 See Anna Harwell Celenza, 'Liszt, Italy, and the Republic of the Imagination', in *The Cambridge Companion to Liszt*, ed. Kenneth Hamilton (Cambridge, 2005), pp. 3–38.

22 Francesco Petrarch, ed. Sabrina Stroppa, *Canzoniere* (Turin, 2011), 134, 1–4 (Liszt knew this poem as *Canz.* 104, having followed an older ordering of the poems).

23 Ibid., pp. 9–14.

24 Rosa was represented by a poem mistakenly attributed to him.

25 Petrarch, *Canzoniere*, 35. Hayden's version is HoB 24b:20; and Schubert set Friedrich Schlegel's translation of this poem (as Sonnet 2).

BIBLIOGRAPHY

A NOTE ON FURTHER READING

For the those who wish to explore the vast scholarship on Petrarch, two recent volumes serve as excellent points of departure: Albert Russell Ascoli and Unn Falkeid, eds, *The Cambridge Companion to Petrarch* (Cambridge, 2015), and Victoria Kirkham and Armando Maggi, eds, *Petrarch: A Critical Guide to the Complete Works* (Chicago, IL, 2009). For readers of Italian, Ugo Dotti's *Vita di Petrarca* is essential, as is Karlheinz Stierle's *Francesco Petrarca* for readers of German. The Bibliography below is not exhaustive and does not represent all the work cited in the References.

Ascoli, Albert Russell and Unn Falkeid, eds, *The Cambridge Companion to Petrarch* (Cambridge, 2015)
Baron, Hans, *Petrarch's 'Secretum': Its Making and Meaning* (Cambridge, MA, 1985)
Bausi, Francesco, *Petrarca Antimoderno* (Florence, 2008)
Bernardo, Aldo S., *Petrarch, Scipio, and the* Africa: *The Birth of Humanism's Dream* (Baltimore, MD, 1962)
Bianchi, Luca, *Il vescovo e i filosofi: La condanna parigina del 1277 e l'evoluzione dell'aristotelismo scolastico* (Bergamo, 1990)
Billanovich, Giuseppe, *La tradizione del testo di Livio e le origini dell'umanesimo*, 2 vols (Padua, 1981–)
—, Giuseppe, 'Il Virgilio di Petrarca. Da Avignone a Milano', *Studi Petrarcheschi*, n.s./2 (1985), pp. 15–52
Colish, Marsha, *Medieval Foundations of the Western Intellectual Tradition* (New Haven, CT, 1997)

DeRidder-Symoens, Hilde, ed., *Universities in the Middle Ages*, vol. 1,
    in *A History of the University in Europe*, ed. W. Ruegg
    (Cambridge, 1992–)
Dotti, Ugo, *Vita di Petrarca* (Rome, 2004)
Duffy, Eamon, *Saints and Sinners: A History of the Popes* (New Haven,
    CT, 1997)
Fubini, Riccardo, *Humanism and Secularization: From Petrarch to Valla*,
    trans. M. King (Durham, NC, 2003)
Gray, Hannah H., 'Renaissance Humanism: The Pursuit
    of Eloquence', *Journal of the History of Ideas*, 24 (1963),
    pp. 497–514
Hadot, Pierre, *Philosophy as a Way of Life: Spiritual Exercises from Socrates
    to Foucault* (Oxford, 1995)
—, *The Inner Citadel: The* Meditations *of Marcus Aurelius*
    (Cambridge, MA, 2001)
Hankins, James, 'Teaching Civil Prudence in Leonardo Bruni's
    History of the Florentine People', in *Ethik – Wissenschaft oder Lebenskunst?*
    Modelle der Normenbegründung von der Antike bis zur frühen Neuzeit, ed.
    Sabrina Ebbersmeyer and Eckhard Kessler (Berlin, 2007),
    pp. 143–57
Hobbins, D., 'The Schoolman as Public Intellectual: Jean Gerson and
    the Late Medieval Tract', *American Historical Review*, 108 (2003),
    pp. 1308–37
Kennedy, William J., *Authorizing Petrarch* (Ithaca, NY, 1994)
Kirkham, Victoria and Armando Maggi, eds, *Petrarch: A Critical Guide to
    the Complete Works* (Chicago, IL, 2009)
Kristeller, Paul Oskar, *Renaissance Thought and its Sources* (New York,
    1979)
Küpper, Joachim, *Petrarca: das Schweigen der Veritas und die Worte des Dichters*
    (Berlin, 2002)
Lubac, Henri de, *Exégèse médiévale: les quatre sens de l'Écriture* (Paris, 1959–)
Maccarrone, Michele, *Vicarius Christi: Storia del titolo papale* (Rome, 1952)
Mann, Nicholas, *Petrarch* (Oxford, 1984)
Mazzotta, Giuseppe, *The Worlds of Petrarch* (Durham, NC, 1993)
Musto, Ronald G., *Apocalypse in Rome: Cola di Rienzo and the Politics
    of the New Age* (Berkeley, Los Angeles, and London, 2003)
Nolhac, Pierre de, *Pétrarque et l'humanisme*, 2 vols (Paris, 1907)

Petrarch, Francesco, *Africa*, ed. and trans. Bernhard Huss and Gerhard Regn (Mainz, 2007)

—, *Canzoniere*, ed. Sabrina Stroppa (Turin, 2011)

—, *La Collatio laureationis*, ed. Giulio Cesare Maggi (Milan, 2012)

—, *Epistulae metricae / Briefe in Versen*, ed. and trans. Otto and Eva Schönberger (Würzburg, 2004)

—, *Le familiari*, ed. Vittorio Rossi (Florence, 1933–68; re-edition, Florence, 1997), 4 vols

—, *Le familiari: Familiarum rerum libri*, ed. Vittorio Rossi and trans. Ugo Dotti (Racconigi, 2004–9), 4 vols

—, *Invectives*, ed. and trans. David Marsh (Cambridge, MA, 2004)

—, *Lettera ai Posteri*, ed. and trans. Gianni Villani (Rome: Salerno, 1990)

—, *Letters of Old Age*, trans. Aldo Bernardo (New York, 2005), 2 vols

—, *Opere di Francesco Petrarca*, ed. Emilio Bigi (Milan, 1963)

—, *Opere latine*, ed. Antonietta Bufano (Turin, 1975), 2 vols

—, *Petrarch's Lyric Poems*, ed. and trans. Robert M. Durling (Cambridge, MA, 1978)

—, *Petrarch's Testament*, ed. and trans. Theodor Mommsen (Ithaca, NY, 1957)

—, *Prose*, ed. Giuseppe Martellotti (Milan, 1955)

—, *Secretum meum – Mein Geheimnis*, ed. and trans. Bernhard Huss and Gerhard Regn (Mainz, 2013)

Petrucci, Armando, ed. and trans. Charles M. Radding, *Writers and Readers in Medieval Italy* (New Haven, CT, 1995)

Quillen, Carol Everhart, *Rereading the Renaissance: Petrarch, Augustine, and the Language of Humanism* (Ann Arbor, MI, 1998)

Rico, Francisco, *El sueño del humanismo* (Madrid, 1993)

Rizzo, Silvia, *Ricerche sul latino umanistico* (Rome, 2002)

Stierle, Karlheinz, *Francesco Petrarca: ein Intellektueller im Europa des 14. Jahrhunderts* (Munich, 2003)

Wilkins, Ernest Hatch, 'The Coronation of Petrarch', *Speculum*, 18 (1943), pp. 155–97

—, *Life of Petrarch* (Chicago, IL, 1961)

—, *Studies in the Life and Works of Petrarch* (Cambridge, MA, 1955)

Witt, Ronald G., *In the Footsteps of the Ancients: The Origins of Humanism from Lovato to Bruni* (Leiden, 2003)

Zak, Gur, *Petrarch's Humanism and the Care of the Self* (Cambridge, 2010)

ACKNOWLEDGEMENTS

It is a pleasure to thank Victoria Fanti and Alyssa Falcone, for their help in editing, and Anna Harwell Celenza, who read numerous versions of this book. Unn Falkeid, Timothy Kircher and Ronald G. Witt generously read this book in draft and provided much helpful commentary. This book is dedicated to Karl Kirchwey, like Petrarch a magnificently humane poet, who has inspired me since we were colleagues together in Rome some years ago.

PHOTO ACKNOWLEDGEMENTS

The author and publishers wish to express their thanks to the below sources of illustrative material and/or permission to reproduce it. Some locations are given here in the interests of brevity.

From Archivio Storico Civico e Biblioteca Trivulziana, Milano MS 905 (Petrarch, *Rime; Trionfi*): 20 (fol. IV) (photo © Comune di Milano – all rights reserved); from Biblioteca Ambrosiana, Milan MS A 79 inf. (the 'Ambrosian Virgil'): 4 (fol. 54r), 5 (fol. IV) (photos © De Agostini Picture Library); from Biblioteca Apostolica Vaticana, Rome MS Vat. Lat. 3197 (Petrarch, *Canzoniere*): 27 (fol. 16v) (photo © 2017 Biblioteca Apostolica Vaticana, reproduced by permission of the Biblioteca Apostolica Vaticana, with all rights reserved); from Biblioteca Civica Queriniana, Brescia MS Inc. G V 15 (Petrarch, *Canzoniere e trionfi*): 7 (fol. 33v), 8 (fol. 7r) (photos Alfredo Dagli Orti/Art Resource, New York); from Bibliothèque Municipale, Cambrai (MS B+239 (229)) (Petrarch, *De Remediis utriusque Fortunae*): 21 (fol. 5r) (photo Médiathèque d'Agglomération de Cambrai – cliché CNRS/IRHT); from Bibliothèque Nationale de France, Paris MS Français 239 (Boccaccio, *Decameron*): 14 (photo Bibliothèque Nationale); from Bibliothèque Nationale de France, Paris MS Ital 548 (Petrarch, *Canzoniere*): 15 (fol. IV), 23 (fol. 11r) (photos Bibliothèque Nationale); from Bibliothèque Nationale de France, Paris MS Latin 6069F (Petrarch, *De viris illustribus*): 16 (fol. Av) (photo Bibliothèque Nationale); from Bibliothèque Nationale de France, Paris MS Latin 6802 (Pliny, *Natural History*): 12 (fol. 143v) (photo Bibliothèque Nationale); from British Library, London Harley MS 2493 (the 'Codex Aginnensis', Livy's *Ad urbe condita*): 9 (fol. 2r), 10 (fol. 2r, detail) [photos © The British Library Board]; from British Library, London MS King's 321 (Petrarch, *Canzoniere*): 13

(fol. 1r) [photo © The British Library Board]; Galleria Nazionale delle Marche, Urbino: 1 (photo Scala, Florence (courtesy of the Ministero dei Beni e delle Attività Culturali)/Art Resource, New York)); Galleria degli Uffizi, Florence: 6, 17, 18, 19 (photos Gabinetto Fotografico delle Gallerie degli Uffizi); photo © Andrii Gorulko/Shutterstock.com: 3; Isabella Stewart Gardner Museum, Boston, Massachusetts: 24, 25 (photos © Isabella Stewart Gardner Museum/Bridgeman Images); photo © LianeM/Shutterstock.com: 11; photo MARKA/Alamy Stock Photo: 26; from Petrarch (ed. Vellutello), *Il Petrarcha, con l'espositione d'Alessandro Vellutello di novo ristampato con le Figure a i Triomphi, et con piu cose utili in varii luoghi aggiunte* (Venice, 1547): 2 (photo Division of Rare and Manuscript collections, Cornell University Library, Ithaca, New York – from the Fiske Petrarch Collection); from Staatsbibliothek zu Berlin, MS Hamilton 493 (Petrarch, *De sui ipsius et multorum ignorantia*): 22 (fol. 28v) (photo Bildarchiv Preußischer Kulturbesitz).

INDEX

Illustration numbers are indicated by *italics*.